COLLABORATION
CODE

"There are many books about how women can lead in a world dominated by men, but Carol Mitchell is one of the few to explore how men can lead effectively without dominating. In this buoyant book, she examines how men can be confident without getting cocky, show empathy without becoming weak, and elevate others without undermining themselves."
—ADAM GRANT, *New York Times* bestselling author of
   Think Again and *Give and Take*, and host of the TED
   podcast WorkLife

"Carol Mitchell has conducted outstanding research on both women's and men's leadership. In *Collaboration Code,* she explodes stereotypes that men have lived with for far too long—particularly those that suggest that men do not or should not lead with empathy and compassion. Through compelling stories, she shows how the best male leaders have developed the emotional intelligence so fundamental to inclusive, collaborative leadership, the kind of leadership that creates and sustains the productive workplaces and healthy cultures we need so badly in today's world."
—ANNIE MCKEE, Senior Fellow and Director,
   PennCLO Executive Doctoral Program University of
   Pennsylvania; *New York Times* bestselling author of
   Resonant Leadership and *Primal Leadership*

"*Collaboration Code* is a powerful book that shows how men are demonstrating principles of Athena leadership. Carol Mitchell's research puts a fine point on the skills and approaches of executive men that blend masculine and feminine traits. This is how men can join women to rule the future."
—JOHN GERZEMA, CEO of The Harris Poll; *New York Times* bestselling author of *The Athena Doctrine*

"*Collaboration Code* is a welcomed clarion call for change in the business-as-usual leadership paradigm among men. Through lucid prose, engaging interviews, and savvy cultural observations, Carol Mitchell makes a strong case for empathy and collaboration as the new skillset men need if they are going to lead successfully in the 21st century."

    —ANDREW REINER, author of *Better Boys, Better Men,*
      masculinity researcher, and frequent contributor to the
      New York Times

"Given men currently occupy the majority of leadership roles, Carol Mitchell rightfully shines a light on masculinity norms that hold male leaders back from achieving their potential. *Collaboration Code* provides an extremely useful solution to the issue it raises—a framework for cultivating collaborative male leadership that organizations so desperately need."

    —KATINA SAWYER, PH.D., Assistant Professor of
      Management, The George Washington University
      School of Business, diversity and leadership researcher

"Carol Mitchell is a proven researcher, accomplished organizational observer, and compelling storyteller. *Collaboration Code* provides a powerful leadership roadmap that male leaders can employ to foster trust, set direction, and build team engagement and employee followership in any organization. This illuminating book is a must-read for any male leader who wants to strengthen his leadership agility and effectiveness with others!"

    — RICK KOONCE, Executive Coach and Managing
      Principal, The Huntington-Northstar Group, LLC,
      Executive Coach to the MBA Program at the Wharton
      School, The University of Pennsylvania

COLLABORATION CODE

HOW MEN
LEAD CULTURE CHANGE
AND NURTURE
TOMORROW'S LEADERS

CAROL VALLONE MITCHELL

Post Hill
PRESS

A POST HILL PRESS BOOK
ISBN: 978-1-64293-636-0
ISBN (eBook): 978-1-64293-637-7

Collaboration Code:
How Men Lead Culture Change and Nurture Tomorrow's
Leaders
© 2021 by Carol Vallone Mitchell
All Rights Reserved

Post Hill Press
New York • Nashville
posthillpress.com

Published in the United States of America

CONTENTS

PART THREE: DEVELOPING AND LEADING WITH THE MEN'S NEW LEADERSHIP BLUEPRINT

ACKNOWLEDGMENTS

I thank the executive men who readily shared their stories. You illuminated the qualities that together make a collaborative leader, and it is because of your openness that I could see a fully lit picture. I appreciate your willingness to reflect on your leadership journey, the ups and downs, and who you are and who you have become in those travels. You are the leaders who make better work cultures for all of us. Thank you!

I also thank the remarkable people in Hawai'i who helped me tell the case study story of "the Hub." I am particularly grateful to Ikaika Marzo, Philip Ong, John Stallman, and Lei Mohr for your openness to share your experiences during what must have been one of the most traumatic times in your life. Thank you to all the wonderful people of Hawai'i Tracker and Hot Seat Hawai'i for giving me a front row seat throughout the eruption and aftermath. Special thanks to my friend Bruce Omori for helping me connect to these heroes and for providing insights on people's heritage and the culture. And thank you to my dear friends Melenani Mendes and Kevin Teves for sharing your stories over the years and grounding me in a local's perspective of Hawai'i.

To my many colleagues who helped me clarify what I was trying to say in this book, I am so grateful. I particularly thank Steve Heinen, Michael Seitchik, Rick Koonce, and Glade Holman for the dozens of thought-provoking conversations, for vetting the Men's New Leadership Blueprint, and for reviewing the manuscript for this book. And thanks to Debbi Bromley for studying the Blueprint and developing reflective questions for the reader.

I also thank Anne Dubuisson, the "author whisperer," who has once again helped me capture my thoughts on the page in a way that is clear, authentic, and coherent. Your challenges, questions, and suggestions pushed me to more thoroughly mine my observations, revealing new insights. You've helped me all along this pathway, from clarifying concept to final edits. It has been a wonderful collaboration. I would also like to thank my agent, Leah Spiro and my editors, Debra Englander and Heather King for recognizing the need for this book and bringing it to fruition.

I give special thanks to my colleague Eric Solomon for embracing the messages in this book and sharing how they resonate for you in the foreword. Your openness, honesty, and trust have been an inspiration to me. I am so glad to have you on this journey.

I especially thank my business partner, Pat Schaeffer. Just as you did with my first book, you have been so supportive and patient with me as I have been off doing interviews and hunkered down in my "book cave." And once again your optimism and reassurance have helped me get through all the various hurdles that stood in my way as I pursued writing this book. I am ever grateful to have you by my side. You are a wonderful business partner and cherished friend.

Also, I am particularly grateful to my husband, Ken. You stuck by me as I frustratedly grappled with the issues of male stereotypes, both before and during writing this book. Importantly, you helped me see a different perspective. Your understanding, suggestions, superb editing, and emotional support have been my rock.

FOREWORD

Dr. Carol Mitchell has done it again.

In her first book, *Breaking Through "Bitch,"* Carol tackled the thorny subject of how female leaders can manage unfair gender expectations and still successfully climb the corporate ladder. Now, she has brought her attention to another unspoken crisis plaguing the workplace today: male leadership. This is a crisis because, frankly, male leadership has become synonymous with reinforcing male stereotypes—and, even in recent times, many male leaders simply don't see this as a problem. After reading *Collaboration Code: How Men Lead Culture Change and Nurture Tomorrow's Leaders*, I have a feeling their perspectives may change.

Through her insightful research, Carol has discovered a road map that outlines what the future of male leadership could and should look like. But in order to get there, men need to invest the time to understand what true leadership is and how our ingrained notion of what it means to be a "guy" plays a major role in shaping our own definitions of how to lead. So, Carol's book is as timely as it is deeply affecting.

Anyone who has held an executive role knows that leadership is not a blank slate. Like many of us who "graduate" or simply end up in corporate leadership positions, I never had much training about what being a leader means. There were some basic, sporadic classes about creating win-win environments or managing difficult conversations. But there wasn't much, at least for me, about how to be a leader. So, like many leaders I've worked with, male or female, I winged it.

However, like every human faced with an unfamiliar situation, I had the benefit of collective past experiences and age-old accumulated wisdom. While we don't always know exactly how to act as senior leaders, we have decades of in situ learning, not to mention all those ingrained, unconscious stereotypes to fall back on. As Carol writes:

"For men, leadership effectiveness has been framed in masculine terms, that is, being powerful, tough, and strong…A leader commands attention, doesn't pull punches, leads the troops, calls the shots, crushes the opposition…[and] if men don't lead this way, they may be considered ineffective."

I hate that there is even a tiny grain of truth in her words, but the masculine imagery of sports and military terminology had seeped into my latent understanding of what it means to be a male leader. The fact that I gravitated toward the hyper-aggressive landscape of Silicon Valley only served to reinforce these manly stereotypes. (Vulnerability? What's that?) So, as a newly minted executive, I looked around at the models of leadership closest to me—mostly male, mostly white—and started to compare myself to them. What I found is that I simply don't stack up.

I am a white man, but I don't fit the stereotype, and I've adopted the notable defense mechanism of trying to keep things funny and light when faced with conflict. I can sometimes inspire people, but I don't think anyone has ever called me powerful, tough, or strong. Yet, I am a leader. Some might even say that I'm a successful one because of the places I've worked and the titles I've held. Like all people, I've made missteps—sometimes tremendous ones—but, time and consideration have led me down a different leadership path than my early Silicon Valley role models. I didn't have the language for it, though, until I read Carol's book.

Collaborative leadership—that's what this book is about, and the stories from the men within it resonate because they illuminate multiple paths toward being a modern, effective leader. Better paths, I think.

Despite the growing body of evidence that empathy, listening, and respect in the workplace are more than just nice-to-haves, the reality is depressing. In many organizations, there seems to be an unspoken expectation about what it means to "be professional." What this amounts to is that there is the private version of ourselves—who we are at home, with close friends, or in more contemplative moments—and a public, corporate-facing version.

This duality of self rings truer the higher up the executive ladder we climb. To be a business leader often feels more like a performance than a job, where we're playing a role similar to the actor Carol introduces us to early in *Collaboration Code*. Keep it professional. Stay focused. Don't waver. Be authoritative, no matter how you feel. This is the messy *kabuki* of male leadership as it always has been. Fortunately, we have Carol to introduce us to a more fulfilling potential.

Several of the men's stories in *Collaboration Code* involve a pivotal moment, whether explicitly acknowledged or not. For some, it was the unexpected, outsized presence of strong women in their lives; for others, it was a monumental or traumatic event. I identify with both. I was raised as an only child of a strong, single mother who did her best to encourage me to explore and to be who I truly am. Then, not long ago, I lost my father—my closest friend and confidant—to a tragic, unresolved death. I was in a new leadership role at the time, in a new city, and I didn't understand how complex the grieving process would be.

At work, I faked strength. I tried to convince colleagues that I was worthy of my title by covering up any natural inclination toward kindness, empathy, or vulnerability. But then, something clicked. I was exhausted from performing typically male leadership roles, especially those that nudged me further away from my core. I am now on a journey to being the type of male leader that Carol describes in these pages—one who expresses empathy and shows humility, one who can be vulnerable, one who is inclusive, one who is open to learning.

Just one final thing. Since my dad's death, I have often wondered how aggressively I would have pursued playing the role of a stereotypical male leader, even though I was never very good at it. Does it need to take a traumatic event to choose a different path? Before meeting Carol, I might have said yes. Now, I'm not convinced.

—Eric Solomon, PhD

INTRODUCTION

At a leadership event sponsored by a professional association, the eighty or so attendees seated around round tables were asked to quickly introduce themselves by giving their name and the name of a recent book they had enjoyed. Across the room, one man stood up and called out the name of my first book, *Breaking Through "Bitch."* Someone else from the crowd added, "The author's here." I turned a few shades of red as I smiled and waved from my seat. Then another man said, "When are you going to write the book for *us*?" There was a bit of friendly banter around the room about what would be the title of such a book. A callout for "Breaking Through A-hole" emerged. All good fun. Many times after that incident, I had men approach me to say how much they liked my book and ask when I would be writing the book for them. Just as I had written a book about how successful women lead—how they lead differently than men, how they lead collaboratively—these guys saw a need for a guide to show men how they, too, can lead collaboratively. One man said, "I can't just follow the characteristics in your book. Then I'd be acting like a woman." Hmm, I thought.

My first book defined a set of behavioral skills that successful women leaders have in common. My research and others' shows that women who lead successfully demonstrate characteristics such as empathy, nurturing, and inclusiveness—collaborative traits we expect women to exhibit. Women "round off the sharp edges" of male-associated characteristics by infusing stereotypically female-associated characteristics into their brand of leadership.

Why should I write a book for men? Collaborative leadership is collaborative leadership, right? Can't men incorporate into their leadership skill portfolio the characteristics we tend to associate with women, without "acting like a woman" as the man mentioned above had feared? Apparently, it isn't that simple.

We expect men to be independent achievers, dominant, and ambitious. It used to be that what was expected of a man was the same as what was expected of a leader. Indeed, when leadership was more top-down, men didn't have a disconnect between being a leader and being a man. But in today's business world, we require collaborative leaders, which carries a new set of expectations. And just as successful women have developed a blend of male and female characteristics that balance gender and leadership expectations, men need to develop a unique blend of those attributes for their own balancing act.

So, what changed? Why did I decide to write this book?

I recognized that men were asking for help to figure out how to balance those expectations.

Another factor was that I could see the business landscape was changing. There is an ever-increasing emphasis on innovation and, therefore, a need for collaborative leaders who create a culture of trust, nurture teamwork, and inspire creativity. We need men, not just women, to lead this way.

And then finally, add to the mix the insecurity among some men brought to the fore by the courageous and crucial #MeToo movement. Gender dynamics that were rife in some work environments long needed a major adjustment and reset.

Combined, this new landscape has left some men who've practiced steadfast-authoritative leadership uncertain, apprehensive, defensive, and doubting their effectiveness. This landscape has further changed more broadly with the havoc wrought by the Covid-19 pandemic. The majority of countries with the best coronavirus responses have been led by women. Avivah Wittenberg-Cox wrote, "Generally, the empathy and care which all of these female leaders have communicated seems to come from an alternate universe than the one we have gotten used to." In a *New York Times* article, Jessica Bennett reported that because of the pandemic, the rules have changed. Not only are male leaders allowed to show emotion, it is appreciated.

It is a moment of change, big change, for men in the workplace. Yet there are men who are successfully navigating this world. I decided to seek them out and look into how they were doing it, in much the same way that I looked into how successful women lead.

How do men weather the storms of cultural change as it plays out in our work environments? How do men lead effectively and build healthy professional relationships and healthier work cultures? How do men blend female characteristics into their leadership style while maintaining their masculinity? How do men lead collaboratively as men? These were just some of the questions I sought to answer.

My research began with in-depth, face-to-face behavioral interviews with executive men identified by executive women colleagues as being collaborative leaders. They included CEOs and COOs of healthcare systems and national managed care companies; senior VPs from international companies in the financial services industry, diversified technologies industry, and communications technologies industry; CEOs in non-profit clinical and educational services; a CEO of a major publishing company; and a general counsel from the transportation industry. It was a pleasure and privilege to talk with these men and learn about their lives and their experiences as senior leaders.

What my interviews revealed is a common thread of traits among collaborative male leaders in business who have learned to blend what are considered "feminine" characteristics into their leadership style. Collaborative male leaders have a relative lack of ego and healthy dose of empathy while confidently asserting themselves and driving others to achieve results. They show vulnerability and do not need to prove themselves or look for affirmation. They include others in problem solving and decision making rather than taking independent action. They listen to others instead of talking over them and striving first and foremost to be heard themselves. And they have a passion for developing leaders and continually learning themselves. I took these findings and created the Men's New Leadership Blueprint™, a set of seven behavioral competencies.

This book is organized into three sections. The first section lays the groundwork for understanding the gender-specific issues men face that are in conflict with being a collaborative leader. It opens with a brief examination of the evolution of leadership and the emergence and need for collaborative leadership. Then, it takes a look at the impact of male stereotypes on collaborative leadership and how men overcome them. What follows is a case study of a pop-up, just-in-time organization collaboratively led by men during the devastating 2018 volcanic eruption in Hawai'i. This inspirational and illustrative tale shows the rise and fall of collaboration, lessons learned, and the leadership characteristics demonstrated that are applicable to companies and organizations.

The second section focuses on the Men's New Leadership Blueprint. Each of the seven traits is defined with behavioral examples and supporting excerpts from the stories I heard from the executives I interviewed.

The third and final section focuses on the importance of the Men's New Leadership Blueprint for leading culture change, developing men to lead companies and mentor future leaders in the new and evolving business environment. It identifies experiences that have taught men to be collaborative leaders and offers strategies for building these traits in emerging and existing male leaders and in themselves. It discusses how this new leadership blueprint creates a collaborative culture where teams flourish and innovation thrives, in contrast to cultures created by traditional male leadership where it does not.

It is my hope that this book will help men understand the profile of traits that led to others' success as collaborative leaders and to incorporate these behaviors into their own leadership portfolio. I also hope that men will find this an opportunity to self-reflect on masculinity in the context of leadership, as did the executive men featured in this book, and recognize the power of the feminine characteristics demonstrated in leading collaboratively. Finally, I hope this book inspires men to effectively interact with women *and* men as they mentor their junior colleagues to become the next generation of leaders, and that it illuminates how the work environment can be a comfortably caring place where men and women feel inspired to bring their best selves.

And one more thing—I have a vested interest in maintaining forward progress in our concept of male leadership, not just as a female business leader, but also as a mother of one of the next generation of male leaders. I want a better environment in the workplace for my son—a place where he can focus his intellectual energy collaboratively rather than competitively, and where his empathy and humility are valued as strengths rather than weaknesses.

PART ONE

UNDERSTANDING THE ISSUES MEN FACE LEADING COLLABORATIVELY

CHAPTER 1

Why Collaborative Leadership?

"In life, change is inevitable. In business, change is vital."
—Warren Bennis

Leadership emerges to fit the situation and the environment, and leadership has evolved over time. Sometime very early in human history, the primary role of leadership was defending and protecting territory. Great leaders conquered; they won wars; they protected their people from aggressors. They were also, as far as the historical record indicates, mostly men, hence the leadership characteristics of defend and conquer were aligned with norms of masculinity. Think Alexander the Great, Hannibal, Julius Caesar, King Richard the Lionheart. There are hints, such as female deity figures and other anthropological artifacts, that prior to the male leadership tradition, women were once considered leaders for their power to create and nurture. But the stories that have found their way down through the ages have been those of the victorious, heroic male leader.

Fast forward to the late 19th century. The Industrial Revolution ushered in machinery, factories pumping out product and "titans of industry" displaying that conquering attitude. Think Andrew Carnegie, John Rockefeller, Henry Ford. Authoritarian leaders continued to rule companies in the 20th century—companies where hierarchy kept assembly lines and processes flowing.

In the 20th century, women took over at work for men who were away or died during the world wars. In doing so, they became a presence and power in the workplace. While traditionally male characteristics like mastery, ambition, and "calling the shots" could be exhibited by women in female domains, such as the kitchen, nursery, and garden, without getting men's hackles up, it's in the domains of men, the domain of work, where women expressing those masculine characteristics became an issue. The competition for power—a man's thing in a man's domain—marked a notable shift in gender dynamics.

Women fought a battle at work, trying to act like men because it was those male characteristics that were prized as the qualities of leadership and power. However, professional expertise, authority, and confidence, when expressed by women, were seen as brash and threatening. Years ago, I asked an executive man what the traits of successful female leaders were. He said, "Women have to blend the best characteristics of women with the best characteristics of men minus those we would judge her harshly for." Turned out he was right. The women who actually managed to navigate their way into the seats of power were those who blended in their feminine characteristics with masculine ones, rather than abandoning them. I unpacked this conundrum for women in *Breaking Through "Bitch,"* finding that women who successfully lead balance gender expectations and leadership expectations.

Meanwhile, the industrial, hierarchical age has shifted to a technology, knowledge, and team-based age. The focus on manufacturing and production has shifted to a focus on services. This puts a premium on relationship building and interpersonal skills. What is beginning to distinguish leaders now are those who build collaboration, trust, and engagement, traditionally the bailiwick of women.

> *The focus on manufacturing and production has shifted to a focus on services. This puts a premium on relationship building and interpersonal skills.*

So, there is a shift toward collaborative leadership.

Companies see collaborative leadership as critical in today's highly networked, partnership-oriented business environments. Leaders must foster unity across organizational silos to make decisions quickly, gain cross-functional collaboration, and create cohesive teams. Furthermore, embracing collaboration at the executive level demonstrates to all levels of the organization how they also should approach work in a collective way. It is leaders who create a collaborative culture.

Additionally, there is a call for all leaders to enable innovation. In a 2019 PwC CEO survey, 55 percent of company leaders claimed they were not able to innovate effectively—that there is a skill gap.[1] The Conference Board reported that building an innovative culture is one of the top three concerns of CEOs.[2]

Finally, the #MeToo movement has illuminated the need for leaders to be more emotionally intelligent and to nurture trust. Aggressive, dominating, competitive leaders are being rooted out. Collaborative leadership addresses both the need to

Collaborative leadership addresses both the need to craft innovative cultures and the need to establish trusting work relationships.

craft innovative cultures and the need to establish trusting work relationships.

COLLABORATIVE LEADERS HAVE FEMININE TRAITS

Global studies conducted by John Gerzema, CEO of The Harris Poll, indicated that many qualities of an ideal modern leader are considered feminine.[3] He writes, "We live in a world that's increasingly social, interdependent, and transparent. And in this world, feminine values are ascendant." He goes on to list the traits that emerged as ideal for today's leaders; they include nurturing, empathy, listening, caring about relationships, and inclusive decision-making. Gerzema specifically calls out empathy as a catalyst for innovation.

So, we are now at a time when men are faced with a need to exhibit collaborative characteristics stereotypically associated with women. They need to express the "feminine side" of their masculinity. And I say it deliberately that way. They can't merely express characteristics of women and succeed, just as women couldn't succeed by acting like men. Men must express a unique blend of masculine and feminine characteristics. And in doing so, they can manage the gender expectations we have of them and balance those with the expectations that we now have of our leaders.

Why? Because organizations need collaborative, team-building, innovation-sparking leaders, and it can't be just the purview of women. We need the particular blend of traits that men can bring to the table in order to create a true balance and ideal organizational cultures. Unfortunately, there are both internal and external forces that make it difficult for some men to shift to this collaborative style.

We need the particular blend of traits that men can bring to the table in order to create a true balance and ideal organizational cultures.

CHAPTER 2

Are You "Man Enough"?: The Impact of Masculine Stereotypes on Leadership

"Stripped of the various masks of masculinity, we're free to be who we actually are. We can love. We can find our purpose. We can connect."

–Lewis Howes

In 2017, the American actor, director, and producer, Justin Baldoni, best known for playing Rafael on the award-winning TV series *Jane the Virgin*, gave a compelling TED talk titled, "Why I'm done trying to be 'man enough.'" Baldoni said that through the roles he has played, he got to live inside characters very different from himself. The characters he played "oozed machismo, charisma, and power." Justin certainly looks the part of the macho leading man with his muscular build, chiseled jawline, and good hair. Over time, he realized that there were parallels between the roles he played on stage and the roles he played off stage. He said, "I've been pretending to be a man that I'm not my entire life. I've been pretending to be strong when I felt weak, confident when I felt insecure, and tough when really,

I was hurting." He said he was putting on a show but was tired of performing.

Yes, men have stereotypes they cope with in work and life outside work. They are supposed to be powerful physically, intellectually, financially—all three if possible. Men fight the perpetual battle of gaining status, or at least keeping even with their peers. They should never be vulnerable, much less show that they are.

The pressure to be "man enough" causes men in all walks of life to shirk the parts of themselves others may perceive as being weak—as soft. Feminine-associated characteristics such as empathy, nurturing, connectedness, and vulnerability are in direct conflict with the subconscious messages that boys hear growing up about how to be a man. Baldoni said, "The script that we've been given, that girls are weak and boys are strong, is subconsciously communicated to millions of young boys and girls, just like it was to me. I'm here today to say that this is wrong. This is toxic, and it has to end."

The most inspiring part of Justin's talk for me was a personal story he shared about how difficult it was for him to admit vulnerability with other men and to not "suffer in secret."

He said, "A little while ago, I was wrestling with an issue in my life that I knew I needed to talk to my guy friends about, but I was so paralyzed by fear that they would judge me and see me as weak and that I would lose my standing as a leader, that I knew I had to take them out of town on a three day 'guy's trip' just to open up." Perhaps recognizing men's need to use a shared activity as a vehicle to relate to one another, the audience laughed. He said it took him until the end of the third day to actually talk about his issue.

A female colleague of mine told me a story about two guys who had worked in our company and shared an office for years. One of the men had gone through a difficult divorce during that time. His office mate didn't know until five years after the fact. He actually found out through a female friend in the office. My colleague was incredulous, and we both laughed at the thought of a woman concealing such an important part of her life from an office mate. There are many interesting threads to unravel from this iconic story demonstrating masculine stereotypes.

The divorced man's behavior is instantly recognizable as the symptom of men's reluctance to share their pain. A man hearing this story about the office mates might rationalize it, thinking that it's not appropriate to share personal information with people at work. But many men—and women—chuckle in recognition of men's tendency to keep even significant personal matters bottled up. Another meaningful aspect to the story is that it is a woman who tells the man's clueless office mate about the painful divorce. A woman would characteristically be the one to pick up subtle cues that something was not going well for her colleague, leading her to check in with him. A man might notice, but there seems to be an unwritten pact among men to protect each other's veneer of stoic invulnerability and not hazard putting a chink in the shield. And actually, a man might not want to risk having his own emotional, empathetic reaction that would make him feel vulnerable.

Perhaps showing vulnerability to another man is perceived as putting themselves in a subordinate position. Or maybe it is more about not wanting to hazard the vulnerability of feeling emotion—emotion that must be contained. Emotion that feels too intimate to share with another man.

So, men struggle with exposing vulnerability. They want to live up to the ideal of strength, courage, and independence; to be someone to lean on; to be someone who can keep a cool, reasoned head in the face of emotional turmoil. And because leadership has been associated with men for so long, the definition of leadership has taken on these same ideals—ideals that conflict with vulnerability.

As a woman navigating a career in male-dominated environments of science and management consulting since the mid-'80s, I am painfully aware of the mandates of swallowing emotion, standing tough and confident, and minimizing vulnerability to protect status. For years I kept conversations at an intellectual level, stomached jokes of questionable taste, and distanced myself from other women because I thought that was required to play a man's game. I was very invested in being one of the guys. Several years ago, I realized that I'd suppressed some of the best parts of myself, such as my ability to be a "tuning fork" detecting others' emotions, connecting with them and supporting them. I'd forgotten how to be open and vulnerable, having kept up my guard and worn my armor for so long. I'd denied myself the companionship of other women because I essentially rejected the feminine part of myself.

Some of these realizations came from researching the characteristics shared by women who had made it to the C-suite. To my surprise, they were not suppressing empathy, vulnerability, and "collaborativeness." They were leading in an inclusive way, using "female-associated" traits to build teams, create a culture of trust, and inspire innovation.

Despite the limited headway in pushing aside traditional gender roles, society still sees these traits in leaders as gendered.

People have a hard time not seeing empathy, caring, or nurturing as female, and courageousness, independence, or fortitude as male.

People have a hard time *not* seeing empathy, caring, or nurturing as female, and courageousness, independence, or fortitude as male. Until we remove unnecessary "genderedness," women may corner the market in collaborative leadership, and organizations will miss out on the power of men who are collaborative.

As men work at being collaborative leaders, they are pushing against their own sense of genderedness of these traits, as well as battling those ingrained scripts that Baldoni described in his TED talk. For some men, being strong means don't admit you have a problem; don't admit you don't know what to do; don't admit you're wrong; don't give an inch; take a tough stand and don't listen to others' suggestions.

But I would argue that it isn't just the internal play loop about being a man that may trip up some men in business; it is the culture that stubbornly retains remnants of the old ideals about how men should lead.

For men, leadership effectiveness has been framed in masculine terms, that is, being powerful, tough, and strong. Attributes are identified in terms of sports or military imagery. A leader commands attention, doesn't pull punches, leads the troops, calls the shots, crushes the opposition. This can be a damaging downward spiral leading to obstructive competitiveness and ruined professional relationships, but if men don't lead in this way, they may be considered ineffective. Studies reported in Harvard Business Review have shown that men, even now, are seen as less competent and of lower status when not adhering to masculine norms, such as when they show vulnerability, act nicer, and display empathy.[4]

In my own research, I heard from men that they had felt pressured by other men to be more "firm," rather than being empathetic and inclusive. For instance, instead of aggressively issuing ultimatums, one senior executive coached people with problematic performance. As a result, his boss regarded him as being "too nice." Another male CEO had been criticized by one board member for "asking" people to weigh in instead of taking the bull by the horns, making a decision, and pushing forward.

> *Instead of aggressively issuing ultimatums, one senior executive coached people with problematic performance. As a result, his boss regarded him as being "too nice."*

The pressure of maintaining and increasing status is the number one stress that executive men suffer, according to a study by Deloitte.[5] Apparently, the adherence to traditional male leadership is a very difficult paradigm to shift! But perhaps this is not that surprising considering the times we live in.

Ironically, we are perched at a historically profound place. In the throes of a global pandemic, when it is critical that leaders work collaboratively across borders, we are seeing just the opposite! It has become the "era of strong men;" of "he-men;" of Trump, Putin, and other authoritarian world leaders; of men who ignore or deny the interdependencies of today's world; of men who focus on building power and maintaining a strong independent stance.

We have a global push backward to a masculinity that is extreme, toxic, and sterile of anything remotely feminine. It is the era of superheroes whose musculature continues to get larger than life. (Check out today's beefy action figures versus those from the '80s or '90s. Mark Hamill points out that even his character, Luke Skywalker, is now ripped.) But this bulked up masculinity, idealized to protect and defend us from alien threats, isn't what makes successful companies. Leadership comprised of these characteristics and based on competitiveness only gets one so far. It does not engender collaboration; instead, it creates a risk-averse environment where people spend their workday fearing criticism and ridicule.

Yes, I am worried about men. They are the ones bombarded with pervasive messages about the virtues of amped-up masculinity. They are the ones—some, not all, as we will see when we meet the men of this study—who can't fathom being vulnerable (letting down a defense of "manliness") and incorporating traditionally female traits (perceived as weaknesses). In fact, a few men have doubled down, lashing out at the progress of technology that robs them of jobs, the ones that require heavy lifting, the ones where you work with your hands, the ones where men can be manly. We don't need this masculinity backlash permeating our corporate institutions and pressuring male leaders to be competitive rather than collaborative. Combine this struggle of holding onto traditional masculinity with the culture shift brought on by #MeToo, and you have quite a perplexing and potentially toxic corporate world.

There is a paradoxical situation in business today that adds to this perplexity. While companies need collaborative leaders to increase teamwork, productivity, and innovation, the pressure for businesses to compete and win—an apparent antithesis of collaboration—continues to increase. The technology industry in particular is a hotbed of competition with companies in constant pursuit of the next new product or service. And with the prominence that technology stocks have in the portfolios of big investors, tech companies are also in constant pursuit of increased share value. In Silicon Valley, men are egged on to prove their prowess and leadership with swagger and certainty, showing nary a hint of vulnerability. The climate is one of heightened competition, and the winners, at least in public perception, are the big risk takers. Big egos dominate. Across industries, it is an era of superstar chief executives... almost exclusively men.

So, we have the issue that male leadership has been associated with traditional male traits. Men and women have expectations that men will act in accordance with those traits. We have intense marketplace competition that reinforces competitive behaviors, behaviors that erode teams and trust, shutting down creativity in the workforce and limiting organizations' ability to innovate. With these internal self-pressures and external social forces, men can be at a disadvantage as they work to lead collaboratively. Yet it is men who must push back and lead collaboratively in order to end this stymieing conflict.

Gender stereotypes are pervasive in our society. Most of us were raised with those stereotypes reinforced, as Baldoni discussed. Women have long battled to break free of some female stereotypes that impede their ability to lead and hold power. They have made some progress. Men, on the other hand, have only in recent times seen the need to break free of some male stereotypes. Their battle has just begun.

CHAPTER 3

Volcano Men:
A Case Study of
Collaborative Leadership

"'A'ohe hana nui ke alu 'ia." *No task is too big when done together by all.*

–Hawaiian proverb and pillar principle
in Hawaiian culture

THREE MONTHS OF LAVA

The island of Hawai'i, also known as the Big Island, is the active volcanic part of the Aloha State. Life here has deep roots in tradition, particularly in the rural, southeastern district of Puna where, in the summer of 2018, a volcano erupted where over seven hundred homes were nestled. As locals put it, Pele rose up to claim the land.

Living a life "off the grid" that largely escaped bureaucracy and structure in many ways defined the culture. Some people had lavish homes on up to twenty beautifully-landscaped acres overlooking the ocean. Many had modest accommodations in suburban subdivisions. Still others lived in very rustic conditions off the beaten path in the rainforest. Water supply depended on catchments to collect the plentiful rainfall measured in feet, not inches.

Onto this paradise, Pele propelled hot ash thirty thousand feet into the air and belched two hundred thousand tons of toxic SO_2 gas every day for two months, contaminating those water supplies. She gushed one billion cubic yards of lava, enough to fill three hundred and twenty thousand Olympic-sized pools, covering 13.7 square miles of land up to eighty feet deep over the course of three months. But she also brought factions of the community together as they watched their homes threatened or consumed by the lava. Neighbors helped one another evacuate, marveled at the historic proportions of the eruption, and mourned not only their homes and property, but the loss of beloved beaches and parks where many of them had gathered from the time they were children. Ethnic Hawaiians, multiethnic long-term locals, and more recent settlers unified out of respect for the forces of nature and in an effort to come to terms with their losses and to plan their futures.

One man in the mix, Ikaika, had lived through an earlier eruption that took his family's home when he was six years old. His prominent extended family had lived in the seaside village of Kalapana for generations before the 1990 eruption there. Ikaika, now a grown man with a boat tour business, walked the streets of his current home in the Leilani estates suburban community, viewing the cracks widening in the roads and running through people's yards and the main intersections. He watched them begin to steam and radiate heat like a piping hot grill. He live-streamed his explorations on Facebook, embracing the role of self-designated reporter for the community. He knew that an eruption was about to start and went door to door to tell people it was time to go.

When a 6.9 magnitude earthquake hit, opening space underground along Kīlauea's lower east rift zone, it opened a clear path for lava to feed from the summit toward the suburban subdivisions. The steaming cracks were now spewing lava and erupting more violently, and mandatory evacuation orders were issued. Then for nearly four weeks, lava fountained from several of the twenty fissures at a spectacular one hundred to two hundred feet, sounding like a roaring steam engine. The earth continued to shake with over sixty thousand quakes, forty-four hundred of them over magnitude 3.0.

Being a long-time vacation homeowner in Hawai'i, I paid close attention to these events from my permanent home outside Philadelphia and stumbled upon Ikaika's reports. At first, seeing and hearing his rough-around-the-edges commentary, I thought, "Who is this dude?" But his awe and alarm were so palpable, I couldn't look away. Okay, yes, he was an attractive thirty-something-year-old man with a smile that dazzled, but there was something more here, I thought. Very quickly, others in the area joined him in documenting this profound event, and soon, a battalion of iPhone videographers brought the world into their experience.

Ikaika partnered with Ashley, a community member who was running for a local council seat, to create Pu'uhonua o Puna, "the Hub," to provide shelter and supplies to those who were losing their homes, farms, and businesses to the lava. Pu'uhonua is Hawaiian for "place of refuge," and as such it was where the evacuees went for emotional support as well. Ikaika acquired a vacant lot owned by a member of his extended family. There, Ashley led volunteers to set up a huge tent and tables. As truckloads of supplies arrived, the volunteers sorted donated goods to create a small-scale department store. Ikaika said, "We set up in one afternoon. People donated water, blankets, tents. It was local citizens just taking care of our neighbors, that's all—the bottom line."

Ikaika realized early on, as the quakes continued and fissure upon fissure opened up on suburban streets, that he was out of his depth in regards to communicating what was happening geologically and how to inform his community about upcoming hazards and the implications of all that they were experiencing. He called a long-time friend and colleague, Philip, who had collaborated with Ikaika to bring safe, cultural, historical tours to visitors to the island. Philip, a geologist who trained at Hawai'i Volcanoes National Park, put much of his family life on hold, hopping on board with Ikaika to inform the community about what was happening with the eruption.

Philip watched the tilt meters, earthquake maps, and all the data from the United States Geological Survey (USGS), and interpreted what he observed, helping people understand what to expect. Whether it was which way the lava was headed, when the channelized river of lava was overflowing its banks, or how close it was to the house they had evacuated, Ikaika and Philip were broadcasting minute-by-minute the information people needed. Although Ikaika looked like he was thoroughly enjoying being the star of the show, he yielded the spotlight to Philip's expertise.

"Interesting," I thought, "this is collaborative leadership!" Ikaika and Philip were coordinating their individual skill sets to lead the expansion and operations at the Hub. They were

They were continually in step, building a momentum that drew people into their efforts. There was a notable lack of ego—no effort to individually distinguish themselves.

continually in step, building a momentum that drew people into their efforts. There was a notable lack of ego—no effort to individually distinguish themselves. They were leaders, but acting in unison as a team.

Philip, whom Ikaika affectionately called "Dr. Phil," was the Hawai'i volcano whisperer, with his late-night broadcasts sometimes from the Hub with others, sometimes alone from his back porch where Wi-Fi wasn't strong and the coqui, tree frogs, were singing like birds. He was a comforting voice in the night.

At the Hub, Philip sat at one of the picnic tables most of the day and evening, talking to people and answering questions. He had maps with diagrams that showed where the lava had covered the land, color-coded by date of the flow. He had aerial photos and video from professional photographers who went up at dawn almost every day, flying over the lava flows and ocean entry points. In those helicopter surveys, they also looked to see if so-and-so's house was still there, whose papaya farm or orchid nursery had been taken. They documented the eruption and incorporated the human element—the emotional element.

The intensity and historic importance of this event cannot be overstated. An eruption effusing some half million cubic kilometers of lava through fissures, forming a channelized river of liquid rock racing twenty-five miles per hour eight miles down to the ocean, hadn't taken place at this magnitude here for at least two hundred years. The first fissuring lava fountain opened up in early May, followed quickly by more than twenty other fissures. Pele eventually focused all her energy on one called Fissure 8, pouring out a river of lava to the sea that showed no signs of stopping until early August.

Sometime in late May, John, a biologist and former Park Service Ranger, learned that Ikaika was broadcasting real-time accurate information, and he had his "geologist friend," Dr. Phil, helping him. John and Philip had known each other for years. John sent a message to his friend, "Hey, you're doing a great job. I'm so proud of you." He praised him for getting correct information out to the public amid the noise of inaccurate chatter. Philip thanked him and asked him to come down to the Hub. John had seen that Philip was not getting any sleep, and neither was Ikaika; they needed help.

In Hawaiian social culture, there is a lot of loyalty within the community. You have to vouch for your friends and your sources of information to have them accepted in the circle. Knowing this, John spent a couple of days with Philip at the Hub, Philip introduced him to Ikaika, and John sat in the background on one of their live broadcasts. When Ikaika felt assured that he had satisfactorily vetted him, he said to John with his characteristic flourish, "You're hired; ready to be famous? Your name is Ranger John," followed by his equally characteristic deep laugh.

So began the broadcasts from the Hub featuring "Dr. Phil" and "Ranger John." They covered the events as they happened, explaining what they saw in a way that the official USGS Hawaiian Volcano Observatory was not in a position to do, since communications from USGS HVO are peer-reviewed and debated by the scientists there before a unified message is delivered. HVO had the further burden of Hawai'i Civil Defense filtering what they could and couldn't say to the public.

As a scientist myself and a Hawai'i devotee, I found these live updates riveting. My husband, also a scientist, and I watched—often late at night because of the six-hour time difference between the island and our home—as Dr. Phil and Ranger John discussed the observations and debated what they could possibly mean. They did a few updates using a white board on which they had drawn a cross-section of the volcano showing its inner plumbing, extracted from a USGS report.

We appreciated how they carefully talked it through in layman's terms, without oversimplifying, using lots of great metaphors to describe in a relatable fashion what they were seeing. There was the comparison of the fountaining lava to a bottle of champagne, the pressurized gas spewing the liquid contents out of the bottle. But my favorite was when Philip described the lava delta, where lava was flowing under the solid-ified rock and oozing into the ocean, as a jelly donut. The power of hydrostatic pressure of the still active flow was squeezing the gooey lava out the end.

They were educating people about how to think through the data. This way of communicating demonstrated their propensity to "meet people where they are" and then bring them along in their understanding—a trait of collaborative leaders.

As scientists, we also appreciated that they explained their thinking behind parti-cular hypotheses. They were educating people about how to think through the data. This way of communicating demonstrated their propensity to "meet people where they are" and then bring them along in their understanding—a trait of collaborative leaders.

Meanwhile, Ikaika was becoming a local hero, being recognized, rightly so, for his efforts. The reason for Ikaika's success was his inclusiveness, bringing in people from his network of family, friends, and business associates to help him establish and lead his pop-up lava relief organization. The collaborative efforts at the Hub yielded so much more than a place for people to pick up donated food and supplies. It was a social gathering place. It provided a base camp for the community to come together, both informally and formally, to collectively plan their recovery and their future. It facilitated alliances among a diverse population of people, empowering them to pressure the government to act more quickly toward getting them back to their properties. The inclusiveness of collaborative leadership at the Hub allowed people to engage in helping themselves.

THE VOLCANO MEN

In an effort to put a finer point on my understanding of this collaborative effort, it was time to find out directly what was behind these men's success. My first trip to interview Ikaika, Philip, John, and others was early December 2018, almost four months after the flow had stopped and the bulk of lava had solidified and begun to cool. The air quality on the island was the best it had been in thirty years. No more glowing red skies and volcanic smog.

The devastated landscape of hardened lava was hidden in the jungle, only accessible with a hefty four-wheel drive vehicle and a resident with ID who could pass through the checkpoints. Walking through the rainforest of thick cane grass, palm trees, ferns, tangled vines, and exotic croton shrubs, it was startling to suddenly see the vegetation yield to an enormous moonscape of volcanic rock. Standing on the new lava—a barren expanse of glistening black rock with sheens of metallic blue, silver, and gold in a ropy, twisted, uneven, broken surface—and looking three miles down to the ocean was astounding, other-worldly.

The Hub that was open 24/7 during the eruption was now open only mid-afternoon through early evening on Mondays and Fridays, serving as a community gathering place to share stories and get emotional support. It was also still hosting community potluck dinners. I met Ikaika on a Monday afternoon at the Hub, a week before it closed.

Lei, a longtime resident and community organizer who had filled the role of comforter in chief throughout the life of the Hub, asking people how they were feeling and escorting them to the offering of hot meals, came over to me as soon as I arrived. She immediately engaged me in conversation and wanted to help me. She said, "If you want to talk to Ikaika, you need to grab him now. He disappears." Apparently, Ikaika only came to the Hub occasionally these days, to keep connected with people, but didn't stay long. She said, "Grab a chair, put it next to him, and then you will get his attention." He was talking to an older man, apparently a frequent visitor at the Hub. When I pulled up a chair and said to the frequent visitor, "Hey, do you mind if I steal Ikaika for a few minutes?" he was very gracious, saying, "Of course," and moving over to another gathering of people.

Ikaika, his Hawaiian name meaning strength and perseverance, is a formidable presence at six feet, five-plus inches, with broad shoulders, a large muscular build, and the face of a Hawaiian king. Indeed, I felt a bit like I was in the presence of royalty, although he was so laid back, his personality and warmth sparkled in his eyes, and he had such a hearty, infectious laugh that I got over that initial nervousness.

As I talked with him at the Hub, he was completely deferential to the team he had amassed around him to make this relief effort happen. Although he liked being center stage, it was difficult to get him to talk about what he personally had achieved. He was matter of fact about the whole enterprise from the perspective of his role in founding it and leading it. He explained that he knew what to do because he'd been through it all before.

In April 1990 through February 1991, lava pushed through the town of Kalapana, burying two hundred homes in up to eighty-five feet of volcanic rock; one of those homes was Ikaika's. "Government was totally different then; just grassroots." In other words, the community was on their own. He recreated the grassroots effort he experienced twenty-eight years before, because the government and relief agencies were slow to respond.

I asked Ikaika what the hardest thing was to accomplish. "Getting our government to accept us. The government didn't appreciate what we did. We had push back from day one. County leadership promised parking and light towers the first day the Hub opened. Two days later—cold shoulder." So, similarly to the 1990 Kalapana eruption, Ikaika and his band of community partners had to take matters into their own hands, tapping the web of connections by way of what locals call the "coconut wireless," an informal cellphone-to-cellphone information network, to get the resources they needed.

Perhaps the biggest coup was having World Central Kitchen—a global organization of chefs who step in during humanitarian crises—provide food at the Hub for evacuees. Ikaika said after World Central Kitchen was turned down by the American Red Cross for not being a certified facility, they found out about the Hub from the Salvation Army, who had also turned them down. When World Central Kitchen came to the Hub, Ikaika said, "We told them, 'Yes! We want you!

People need food yesterday.' So, they came, they cooked, and they served meals to hundreds of people."

Then the health department came. "There's a way to go around, over, or through red tape." Ikaika smiled. I pressed Ikaika to explain how he got "around, over, or through" the health department rules about preparing and serving food. Again, the smile. He said, "You know, Hawai'i is a small island, so we all know each other. I have a cousin who works in the health department. When they come down, they give you the paper. Then go 'bye bye;' okay, whatever. Simple as that." Then his deep hearty laugh.

Getting "around, over, and through" red tape seemed to be Ikaika's MO. In another example, Ikaika and his compadres at the Hub wanted people to have their own spaces, little places for families to have some privacy. They decided to build transitional homes, tiny houses. Using local companies, they were able to bring down the costs of wood, carpentry, and painting. They acquired a piece of land from a private property owner willing to let Ikaika and crew "borrow" it.

When I asked if there was a "YES!" fist pump moment, Ikaika said, "No, not really. We're still trying to get people back in their homes—we can't really celebrate because there's still stuff to do. You know, take one step forward, two steps back." When I pressed him about how he was helping to get people back in their homes, I knew part of it involved getting the county to plow through the wall of lava that blocks a highway and an access road to homes that were not taken by the lava but were surrounded by it, like an island, a "kipuka." But I didn't know how he was approaching it.

Again, in a matter-of-fact way he said, "We met with people in the community weekly. Everybody got together to brainstorm. It was getting everybody to think the same about what's our best chances for getting to homes land-locked in lava. We came up with a collaboration—have the government create an easement—and went to the mayor." Ikaika said, "We all came to an agreement."

Ikaika also lined up private contractors to plow a road to

"We met with people in the community weekly. Everybody got together to brainstorm. It was getting everybody to think the same about what's our best chances for getting to homes land-locked in lava."

Pohoiki, one of the lava-locked areas. They were ready to roll if the county didn't come through. Much to everyone's relief, the county did come through. I asked Ikaika what had made the government come around. "Social media. We pushed the issue and since it was an election year, they do stuff they don't want to do." Again, the hearty, knowing laugh. The other power that Ikaika and his team possessed was trust. He said, "Our own community members didn't trust the government agencies, but they trust us."

A few days later, over coffee in the lounge of Volcano House, a rustic lodge on the Kīlauea summit at the rim of the crater, I talked with Philip—"Dr. Phil"—a quiet, thoughtful man with a warm, welcoming smile that radiates in his crinkled eyes. His frizzy black hair, touched with an occasional silver strand, is pulled into a bun at the nape of his neck. He has what he describes as an "international background," starting life in Rio de Janeiro, born to a Chinese father and an American mother.

His father's work took them to England when Philip was in middle school, then North Carolina for high school and college. During college, his parents moved to Switzerland, then

Malaysia and, finally, Thailand. He feels that his exposure to various cultures while growing up tuned him in to the nuances that are woven into any culture. He uses that awareness to understand and work in the community in Hawai'i.

Philip settled in Hawai'i after graduate school, and he recognized early on that he could help educate the tour operators to run their excursions safely rather than going for the sensational and risky business of getting as close to the lava as possible. A dozen or more years ago, he had counseled Ikaika in safe practices, like where on the hardened lava you can walk without the hazard of a foot or whole leg breaking through the crust. Philip said to me, "Just because your house is taken by the lava, doesn't make you a tour guide, right?"

There had been a thirty-plus year lava flow from Kīlauea's Pu'u Ō'ō crater that stopped as this eruption started. During those days, casual enterprises cropped up operated by folks who had no training or scientific background. Philip's approach was to offer free seminars to give all of the tour operators more information and to solicit questions. Philip explains geology and the physics of the volcano plainly, not simplistically. He is insightful and humble, and he is deferential to the local culture, working to "fit in" and be a part of it. He establishes a two-way relationship with his audience, respecting their knowledge and traditions, and making a point of learning from them as they

He establishes a two-way relationship with his audience, respecting their knowledge and traditions, and making a point of learning from them as they learn from him.

learn from him. He has formed an effective bond of mutual respect and affection with people here in Puna.

During spring 2018, Philip was paying close attention to tilt meters around Halemaʻumaʻu (the crater at the summit of Kīlauea), Puʻu Ōʻō, and the earthquake map on the USGS website, as things were obviously changing. When the Puʻu Ōʻō crater floor collapsed on April 30th, Philip knew it would lead to something significant. In the next three days, more cracks opened, a huge pink plume puffed out of Puʻu Ōʻō, and three major earthquakes, one a magnitude 6.9, rattled the island. After the M6.9, the level of the Halemaʻumaʻu lava lake began dropping then eventually disappeared from view, draining into the volcano's complex underground plumbing.

About the photos from professional photographers, Philip said, "I never realized how important those pictures were until they started feeding me the photo information." Because of the aerial photos and videos, Philip could see the level of the lava river, how it surged to the brim of its banks periodically, then subsided. He could see the direction the river would take; he could see what areas and homes were in the crosshairs. He said, "What I really worried about was 'Are the citizens going to get warned?' I thought, 'Somehow it's falling to us to warn people.' That was the most stressful part of it."

Philip had to leave the island for two weeks during the height of the eruption to see family in Thailand. He said he was "totally desperate," because of his concern that, in his absence, no one would be communicating to the community about the progression of the eruption. So when he got a text from John, Philip replied, "Oh my God John, I need help." Philip said to me, "Someone had to be here at the Hub to tell these people what this map means."

When Philip returned from his family visit, he got right back into the hot seat. He talked about tilt meter readings and summit collapse earthquakes at the summit, but more than that, his enormous concern and empathy poured out of his broadcasts as he talked about areas soon to be taken by the lava and what they meant to him, his wife, and children. But he would always add, "I didn't grow up here, so I know this must be hard for you guys who did." His deference to locals and the culture endeared him to them. It reinforced his status as "The Guy" people turned to for information they could trust; he really was one of them.

On another day, I went on a four-hour guided tour with "Ranger John," followed several days later by interviewing him at the offices of Friends of Hawai'i Volcanoes National Park. John is an independent spirit who reports that he lives in a "shack in the jungle" on three acres. He sports a slim, youthful, clean-cut look with thoughtful eyes, a closely trimmed brown beard and mustache, several strands of tiny shells around his neck, and a backward donned baseball cap.

John grew up in Idaho, where he points out there are volcanoes that arose from a hot spot just like the Hawaiian volcanoes but are now dormant. After getting a botany degree at the University of Puget Sound, he bought a one-way ticket to Hilo and eventually became a park ranger and tour guide. Similar to Philip, he is passionate about the ecosystems around the volcano. In fact, the similarity of these two men sparked a mutual friend to invite them for a day of kayaking so she could introduce the two of them.

John shared with me how much stress he had felt during the eruption. Not only was he spending all of his time working with Philip to keep up with the daily changes in the volcanic activity, he had a few friends who had evacuated their homes staying with him in his tiny house. No one slept much. John thought he had to be "the rock" for his traumatized friends.

But when John told me the story about being at the crater rim when the M6.9 earthquake hit, he did not feign a calm demeanor; he spoke rather dramatically and excitedly. "I was tour guide for a group of fifteen guests, all in their sixties and seventies. It was like a movie scape. The sky was gray, and the crater let out a big dust cloud that was slightly pink. You could see the rockslides all around the edges of the crater, and red dust and rock thrown up against this slate gray sky.

"In Hawai'i, an M6.9 is significant, to the point where it is difficult to stand, so the guests were hanging on to each other, hanging onto trees along the edge of the crater. It was like we were just sailing through the air, and you could hear boulders falling out of the cliff edges. One seventy-something-year-old woman walked right up to the edge to get a picture. I was like," John deepened his voice in exaggeration and assumed a rather stern expression, "'Ma'am, please step away from the four hundred-foot cliff.' Then I said, 'Okay everyone, we are just going to ride this out.' We did. Everyone was fine. We went back to Volcano House for pupus, then we got word that the lava lake in the crater was draining and they were evacuating the park."

When John left for Alaska in July to lead a science tour group of Chinese students, he felt relief, although he said he didn't get much sleep there either. Being on what was pretty much a camping trip with teenagers and not conducive to sleep anyway, he was also "wingman" for Philip, listening late at night to his Facebook broadcasts so he could answer the questions that the viewers posted in comments. He wanted to make sure his responses were consistent with what Philip had said.

While John was away in Alaska, he picked up from comments on the video updates that some people were being nostalgic, saying that they wished it was just Philip and/or Ikaika doing the updates, like it used to be. It bothered him, thinking that he was not being accepted by the community. Meanwhile, it was clear to me that while Philip, and more so Ikaika, wore their hearts on their sleeves, John was less demonstrative of his emotions, striking a friendly "professional" stance as he did during our guided hike at the volcano. And it took getting to know him better for me to see how funny, caring, and open his was. So, I could see how in comparison to Philip and Ikaika, some people were not as warm and fuzzy about John.

When John returned to Hawai'i after a month away from all the drama, he realized just how stressful the situation had been there at the Hub. He saw Philip and Ikaika were a little wild-eyed, a little zombie-like, needing sleep. Jumping back into it, he regained a sense of truly being an appreciated part of the team. He remembered a very validating moment before he had left for Alaska. He said, "One day, Ikaika pulled me aside to come sit with him and 'the rest of the boys.' He motioned to the chair next to him and he said, 'How can I ever thank you for what you've done?' It was deep and people witnessed it."

John thought one of the factors in his "outsider" status might have been racially driven. "It was easier for all of Puna to look at Phil than me. I could definitely feel it. Some were slow to validate what I was saying, slow to acknowledge it on a par with Philip's information."

From my perspective, the collaborative broadcasts did not show any tension whatsoever. Instead, I had noted that we had the Hawaiian giant, the non-Hawaiian multinational, and the skinny white guy working together like a well-oiled machine. It was the differences of the three men that captured my attention, the fact that they were able to gel as a collaborative leadership team despite their different backgrounds and personal styles.

John said it was Ikaika's personality that overcame the issues around differences, and that was baked into the philosophy at the Hub. The Hub was neutral ground; differences were pushed aside because, as Ikaika told me, "We are all in the same boat." John said ethnic Hawaiians, and Ikaika in particular, are genuinely inclusive. Philip pointed out to me that the old Hawaiian families are like that; they hold onto those traditional Hawaiian values.

Both Philip and John told me that Ikaika can put his arm around someone, endorsing them, and the local crowd then readily accepts them. "That's what was magical about Ikaika," John said, "that sense of inclusion from him. The people needed a hero—at a personal level. They needed it from all of us. Ikaika was a symbol of strength. Emergency drew us together; that was our strength."

> *Ikaika can put his arm around someone, endorsing them, and the local crowd then readily accepts them. "That's what was magical about Ikaika," John said, "that sense of inclusion from him."*

COLLABORATIVE LEADERSHIP LESSONS FROM THE HUB

The Hub, an ad hoc organization created during a chaotic humanitarian crisis, was like an amplifier turning up the volume on behaviors. It served as a business fable, highlighting lessons applicable to the corporate world. The leadership characteristics demonstrated by this male trio are consistent with those of the collaborative leaders defined in the next chapter and described at length in subsequent chapters of this book.

Tempering Ego

Ikaika, Philip, and John all have healthy egos. But during the catastrophic days of the eruption, these men put aside their egos and worked together. There was no pecking order and no jockeying for control. This was essential to leading collaboratively and to effectively managing the crisis. Ikaika loves the spotlight but soon relinquished it to Philip and then John. Philip treasures his reputation as the expert, "The Guy," but pulled in John, endorsing him as a peer colleague. John values being recognized for his own knowledge and insights but deferred and presented a united front with Philip. They each subjugated themselves to the mission of the Hub and to the greater good of the whole community.

Ikaika, living this island's values of humility, responsibility, and to do what you were born to do, didn't have much of an obstacle to overcome regarding ego. He acted as if, of course he would do this. He would do this because it is a responsibility that was handed down to him through the generations. It turns out he is literally Hawaiian royalty, the bloodline of King Kamehameha! Perhaps because of his leadership and his regal pedigree, he is seen as a future leader of the Hawaiian community. Some refer to him as "the mayor" of the region, and he may indeed be elected. But Ikaika doesn't beat his chest about this honorific; he just shrugs and says he does what he was meant to do.

Ikaika was in a privileged position; he was born into the Hawaiian "leadership pipeline." Seen as a community leader, adored by most, family to many, he had no need to prove himself or gain endorsement. So he may have had less of a hurdle to clear to collaborative leadership than did Philip and John. He was comfortable in his own skin and secure in his status, so it may have been easier for him to temper his ego. Ikaika did not need to be seen as "the expert." He knew that he was out of his depth regarding the science of the volcano, and in order to endorse his leadership team, he had to show his confidence in them by stepping aside. Instead, Ikaika's role was orchestrator in chief and steward of his community.

The pre-western community/family culture of Hawai'i has its fingerprints all over this. Ikaika not only has lineage status and is therefore secure in his leadership role, but he is immersed in the old Hawaiian culture where getting things done is a well-coordinated group effort. No one is more important than anyone else. In the old days, men and women had different but equal roles and status. Families were, and are, extended and expansive; everyone in the clan is afforded the same level of care, respect, and responsibility. So when crisis happens—the "coconut wireless" kicks in—everyone is on it.

John probably had the biggest challenge in tempering ego. He did not have the beloved local expert status of Philip and may have been seen as challenging that status. Although John was a Puna resident with most of his friends evacuated or profoundly affected by the eruption, he had no family there, no kids to go to school with other kids in the community, as Philip did. He felt like Philip's understudy, and not a welcomed one at that. So, unlike Ikaika and Philip, he did have something to prove—a tough position when trying to temper ego.

The importance of being self-aware and fitting in to the culture of the group is another highlight of this collaborative leadership story. You cannot do this if you do not temper ego. Ikaika didn't even have to think about it; it was his culture. Philip and John did have to think about it and work to fit in, and that required pushing their egos aside and focusing outside themselves.

Philip, in particular, downplayed his de facto expert status and focused on facilitating discussion with the community, soliciting their experiences and perceptions while sharing his. As the science guy, he could have been intimidating, but he presented information and his perspective in such a purpose-fully down-to-earth manner that people gravitated to him.

Empathy, Listening, and Respecting All

The Hub was a refuge and an emotional support. The leaders there recognized that their success in providing support to evacuees depended on their ability to be empathetic. They had to face the powerful emotions of the people displaced by the lava who were losing their land, homes, and businesses. Philip and John listened to their stories—even as they focused on informing and educating them, they would pause, deferring to the evacuees' need to talk through their experience. Their empathy bonded them with the community.

A guiding value at the Hub was respecting all. Ikaika insisted that people show respect for one another and not let different ethnicities, socio-economic groups, and political affiliations splinter the collaborative operation. His focus on respecting all, listening, and empathy set the tone and was the glue that unified the leadership team and the evacuees.

Ikaika's awareness and empathy were evident when he sensed that John may have felt like and been seen as an outsider, and helped John by endorsing him publicly and letting him do the live broadcast—first in conjunction with him while Philip was out of the country, and then alone. Ikaika further endorsed John by literally pulling him into his inner circle at the Hub, having him sit next to him, and then thanking him publicly in front of "his boys." Corporate leaders can take a page out of Ikaika's playbook by paying attention to endorsing diverse people on their teams to help them be fully accepted.

Ikaika's actions may have leveled the playing field, but it was John's efforts, spending endless hours at the Hub talking with and listening to evacuees, supporting Philip and Ikaika, and showing how invested he was in being a part of the community, that made him a valuable member of the leadership team.

Cultivating Shared Accountability

Significant in this story, making it an allegory for corporate America, is the collaborative leadership among a diverse group of people. Ikaika didn't just have his family and extended family (Hawaiians, locals) involved. He established a leadership team with each member having a role: Ikaika as orchestrator in chief, Philip as the science guy, and John as the teacher. They depended on each other and worked together like a precision relay team.

In a corporation, leaders have to bring in people who are different, not part of the family as it were, and trust them and share power with them. They have to deliberately endorse those who are different to help them be accepted by the organization.

Collaborative corporate leaders create leadership teams—circles that have meaningful connections with one another. It's different from the male paradigm of the "old boys' network" of "you scratch my back, I scratch yours." That paradigm focuses on status and pecking order. You "call in your chits," you give to get, you don't let people get too many legs up on you. Rather, collaborative leaders have a different paradigm. Their value is on the strength of relationships, not status, and on responsibility to the group. It is more egalitarian, and less about ego.

Importantly, in corporate America or in Puna Hawai'i, to deal with a crisis as magnificently as Ikaika and his network did, you have to already be a collaborative leader with the emotional capital, trust, and enthusiastic collaborators at the ready to help you attack the problem. Ikaika had an extensive network of family and friends. The tight connections were already established, and he was able to pull others into that strong network.

Driving Mission and Meaningfulness

Having a strong purpose and mission propels company success. In a crisis situation such as this, it comes with the territory. Ikaika, Philip, and John were passionately committed to getting the community through the extraordinary circumstances of their homes and livelihoods being buried in as much as 180 feet of lava. They were sure that if they didn't step up to the plate to lead the effort, circumstances would be dire and lives could be lost. And importantly, they engaged the evacuees as a force in driving the mission and meaningfulness. People who had lost their homes and were receiving food and other provisions at the Hub also voluteered their services to help run its 24/7 operation.

The eruption was not cast as a war against an enemy, but rather, a shared problem to be solved collaboratively. Ikaika led regularly-scheduled community meetings at the Hub to come up with a strategy to build and repair roads and propose a plan to the county government. It was a prime example of collective problem solving and decision making that energized people and increased the evacuees' sense of self-efficacy and control. This collaborative approach switched people's perspectives away from being victims, and it bridged differences among the group. As Ikaika said, "Everybody's in the same boat." Keeping their collective eye on the ball helped them endure the drama of their circumstances.

Engaging people in the mission and lifting the collective spirit sometimes took the form of a party. The community dinners often featured live music, compliments of Ikaika, a slack key guitarist, and his guitar-playing family and friends. I'd watched him perform on stage with others, each of whom took turns doing short solos. I wondered if it was a competitive thing, each trying to outdo the other. You know, a guy thing. He said, "It's a family tradition. Each family has its own style. You can show off your style to say, 'This is where I come from.' It's not really a competition; it's a sharing."

And it's not a guy thing; his great grandmother played slack key guitar. Ah, so it's really a nurturing thing, I thought. Makes sense that he would play slack key for people at the Hub. Just as I was feeling warm and fuzzy about that, Ikaika grinned and said, "I like to play because the music makes the beer taste way better." Then he gave me one of those characteristic hearty laughs.

THE END OF COLLABORATION?

I returned to Puna mid-February 2019, six months after the last of the lava erupted and two months after the Hub held its last community dinner and struck camp. Ikaika was away focusing on his music. Philip and John were each off doing their own thing—John with the National Park, Philip with the Hawai'i Tracker Facebook group. There was one more person I needed to talk to: Lei, the comforter in chief.

Lei, who had helped me make a connection with Ikaika at the Hub for my interview, was eager to point out to me what a significant role "unsung heroes" had in the success of the Hub, several of whom were women. In fact, she wanted to make sure that I didn't paint Ikaika as a hero. The network of people who led this effort led it together; Ikaika could not have done it alone. This of course fit precisely into my thesis.

To my dismay though, I came back to find something was no longer there. I know that physically, the Hub was no more, but I had expected to see evidence of the collaborative web that created that oasis.

Lei was participating in meeting after meeting in Hilo, working on various committees, helping out the Hub's cofounder, Ashley, who was now their local councilwoman, all in efforts to get affordable housing and to ensure that volcano recovery money was channeled appropriately. The two women leaders had a shared goal. They were working collaboratively with the community to propose specifically what was needed, just as Ikaika had done at the Hub.

But among the other Hub leaders, there was no longer a big shared goal or the fervor of mission to bring them together and forget their differences. Now that the need to inform the community about the volcano's wrath had dissipated, it became clear that two of these men were focused on different goals. John wanted to educate, dig into the science, talk about the magma movement underground, and speak truth. Philip wanted to reassure Puna, not be overly provocative talking about data implications that could stimulate post-traumatic stress disorder.

With the shared purpose gone and individual goals more obvious, the desire to protect ego and reputation erupted. Philip wanted to protect his position as the trusted source of information, the volcano whisperer. John wanted to protect his status as a legitimate scientist and teacher. Each now trying to protect their own standing, they were working at cross purposes. It escalated into a conflict between the collaborators and friends.

With the shared purpose gone and individual goals more obvious, the desire to protect ego and reputation erupted.

The eruption provided a spotlight for each of these men. They thrived on it, each in their own way. When Pele was finished with her geological masterpiece, the lights went out and their hits of adrenaline stopped. The Volcano Men broke up, looking for another spotlight and source of invigoration. Ikaika found his performing slack key guitar and running for mayor. For Philip, his limelight was leading live feed broadcasts via the Facebook group Hawai'i Tracker, which had grown from four thousand to fifty-one thousand members during the eruption. John found his through his work with the national park doing presentations, tours, and outreach.

Though truth be told, I don't think any of them could match the spotlight and shot of adrenaline they got from the eruption. However, collaborative leadership forged in a time of crisis—real or hyped—can be tenuous. The enormity of the mission covers up differences, smooths them over, but that is hard to sustain when the crisis ends.

Herein lies another important lesson that corporate America can take from the Hub. Collaborative leadership, particularly among men, requires strong shared goals that forge strong relationships. Lose that focus, and egos emerge to get in the way of empathy and self-awareness, relationships erode, and the bond that holds together a powerful collective force is broken. You don't need an erupting volcano to make men collaborative leaders—though I've sometimes wondered if it doesn't take extraordinary circumstances for men to put aside their egos— but you do need a strong purpose, a shared passion, and a little fire under their feet.

PART TWO

MEN'S NEW
LEADERSHIP BLUEPRINT

CHAPTER 4

A New Model for Men's Leadership

"If you are under the impression you have already perfected yourself, you will never rise to the heights you are no doubt capable of."

–Kazuo Ishiguro

My quest to find the unique code for collaborative men's leadership success revealed a balanced conglomerate of male and female associated traits, which I had expected. Yet what I didn't expect was that with every interview, I began to see the professional landscape in a new and positive light. Successful, collaborative male leadership wasn't just happening in industries seen as caring and nurturing, such as health care; it was happening in the financial industry, in technology industries, in transportation, and in publishing. The style of leadership that I knew to be most effective for women, and for today's innovation-seeking organizations, was being reinforced by men.

I took the same rigorous research approach as I had done for *Breaking Through "Bitch"* by conducting in-depth behavioral interviews to identify a specific set of characteristics and behaviors that define a successful collaborative male leader. The men I interviewed told me stories about high points and low points as leaders, which provided much of the data for my analysis and conclusions.

The executive men that you will meet in these pages are individuals with their own unique personas. That data came from my interactions with them: how they presented themselves, how they treated me, what they chose to share, how they related their stories to me, how tuned in they were to our discussion. Before we discuss the characteristics of the Men's New Leadership Blueprint, which is a composite based on the group as a whole, let me introduce you to them as individuals. While the names are fictitious, the people are real, although I have avoided providing details that might make them identifiable.

THE MEN BEHIND THE BLUEPRINT

Andrew, CEO of a publishing company, is part of a wealthy family and spent much of his youth in a rural area, though he is now a New Yorker. He is a friendly, wiry, energetic man in his early sixties. He has a solicitous, warmhearted style, quickly putting people at ease. He met me at the top floor reception desk, waving me on to follow him down the hall to his office. Just as he did, the fire alarm blared; an announcement was made that a fire drill would begin, and everyone had to leave the building. With a conspiring glance, as if we were cutting class and sneaking off to the cafeteria, he walked a bit faster and quietly said, "Come on. Don't want to get caught." Andrew is understated and casual, with a quick wit and mischievous humor.

Charles, CEO of an educational services organization, is a man of color in his early forties who grew up in an inner-city environment. He has a charismatic presence; with striking good looks and impeccable dress, he radiates enthusiasm for his mission of providing high quality educational opportunities for disadvantaged youths. As a panelist in a strategy and leadership session I attended, he dazzled the audience with his passion and perspectives on developing leaders and was flocked by dozens of people at the end of the program.

Craig is a business unit head and senior vice president of an information technology giant in his early sixties who spent much of his life in the Chicago area. His humility was evident throughout our interview, as this very accomplished leader repeatedly said how honored he was to be a part of my research and was curious about what I was learning. He talked about his days in a clinical testing lab job which led him to work on IT systems and eventually lead those system implementations. Since I also started my career as a lab scientist, it provided common ground for us, and I quickly felt a connection with him.

Dane, a senior VP in technology and communications in his early fifties, grew up in the Midwest. He went into the Marines right out of high school, where he received technology training before leaving active duty and getting his bachelor's degree in organizational management as a part-time adult student. His career trajectory consisted of multiple IT positions throughout the country. He is still on the move. Right before I spoke with him, he had just returned from a two-week tropical vacation, a break before moving to his "next thing."

Daniel is the CEO of a national managed care services provider in his mid-sixties who is very fit and looks much younger. He grew up in a middle-class suburb and has an Ivy League education. My interview with him felt more formal than the others, taking place in a conference room rather than his office. He is friendly, though a bit guarded, preferring to converse on an intellectual rather than personal level. Regardless, he is an upbeat, positive person.

Emmet, the CEO of a hospital system, is a man in his late forties who grew up with blue-collar parents. His polite manner and accent are in keeping with his southern background. Talking with him truly is a dialogue; he listened carefully to my questions and comments. His bright optimism about his industry and his career were refreshing.

Kevin, a senior vice president in a multi-entity healthcare organization who is in his late forties, began his career as an occupational therapist, working primarily with stroke victims. He has spent his entire career in his home state, deliberately wanting to help people "in my own backyard." When I interviewed him, he was in the throes of reorganizing the system and anticipating a merger or takeover, yet he was positive, relaxed, and delighted to talk to me about his leadership experiences.

Neil, CEO of a healthcare system, was raised by a physician and a nurse in an Irish family in the suburbs. He is a lively guy with a good sense of humor in his late fifties who I'd say is a "physician whisperer," with his ability to finesse the oftentimes difficult relationships with the doctors in the system. Our interview went long, even though he had a lunch meeting. He asked his assistant to send a message that he was running twenty minutes late, then turned to me and said, "I can spend a little more time talking about this topic."

Nick is general counsel of a public transportation company who grew up in an Italian family and community. He is in his late fifties with a youthful, impish smile that conveys kindness and charm. In his off time, he is an athlete, rigorously training for long-distance cycling events. He has a deep commitment to family. Having just lost his younger brother to a sudden and aggressive cancer, he started a fund to help his two preteen nieces save for college. He is thrilled about the recent birth of his first grandchild, which is helping in his healing process.

Patrick is a business unit president of a manufacturing giant who grew up in a working-class Irish community in the suburbs. He is a modest, open man in his early fifties, whose self-reflection has put him in touch with who he is and how he affects others. His empathetic nature was shaped by the many tragedies he has experienced. As a young child, he lost his father through divorce, then lost his high school girlfriend to cancer and his first child at birth. He readily shares his concern about balancing work and time with his family.

Paul is CEO of a nonprofit regional provider of behavioral and educational services in his mid-fifties. A former social worker, he served as executive director, then senior vice president for a for-profit managed care company for twenty-five years prior to taking his current CEO role five years ago. He started out as an organic farmer, first in Virginia, then in Maine, running a roadside vegetable stand and cut-your-own Christmas tree farm with hayrides. Paul told me that, even now, he reflects back to what he learned being a farmer and applies it to how he runs his organization and cares for his people there.

Rafael, CEO of a biological services organization, is a man of color in his mid-forties who grew up in Latin America in an affluent family that relocated to the US when he was a teen. He is calm, reflective, and a self-described romantic. I interviewed him over dinner at his favorite local restaurant, an Italian trattoria known for its popularity with the Rat Pack, where he eagerly told me about his fairy-tale engagement and upcoming wedding.

Stephen, CEO of a human services organization, is in his mid-sixties with a tireless dedication and passionate enthusiasm for his work. He takes personally the fight for regulations that will improve the industry, actually tearing up in frustration when talking about it during our interview. He takes pride in being able to go toe-to-toe with physicians despite not being an MD. He says he will retire in a couple of years, but his personal engagement is so strong I think it will be difficult for him to do so.

Tim is CEO of a statewide community health center system in his late fifties who grew up in a semirural area outside Chicago. He is a second generation American of Russian and Romanian parents and was the first in his family to get his MD. He is a kind, considerate person with a quiet voice and calm demeanor. He worked as a science writer in New York City for a year before going to medical school. But his most transformative experience was spending two months of medical school in Guatemala, serving as the only doctor on a large coffee farm. After that he was drawn to providing health care to minorities who have traditionally been underserved.

Vincent heads up global capital markets in a large financial institution. He started out on the retail side of the business right out of college and filled in as a teller, loan officer, or whatever was needed in the dozens of branches in his state. He is a shy, self-described introvert in his fifties, who pushes outside his comfort zone to connect with people in the company. I could tell, as we sat at the round table in his office sipping our bottled water, that he was initially pushing himself to relax and be open with me, and he did.

□□□

The experience of meeting these men and hearing their stories was inspiring. I gained a level of appreciation of men, and confidence in them, that I had not had before. They, and men and women like them, are the leaders who drive the best business results, create healthy organizational cultures, and change the face of leadership. They create an environment where other collaborative leaders—including, and in particular, women—can thrive.

From the analysis of my interviews with these collaborative male leaders, I distilled seven characteristics, grouped into two sets.

One set is the foundational traits and underlying values that give one the personal efficacy to lead collaboratively. These characteristics are: Tempering Ego, Empathy, Listening, and Respecting All.

The other set is the collaborative organizational leadership abilities built on that foundation. These are: Driving Mission and Meaningfulness, Cultivating Shared Accountability, and Developing Future Leaders.

Together, these are the behavioral skills of the Men's New Leadership Blueprint.

I checked for face validity of these findings with a review board comprised of male colleagues who are executive coaches, business leadership professionals, and strategy consultants. They found these characteristics to ring true to what they experience personally and to what they see with men who are clients and colleagues in leadership.

MEN'S NEW LEADERSHIP BLUEPRINT™

Personal Efficacy

Tempering Ego

Collaborative male leaders show strong self-assuredness that is a blend of confidence and humility. They go out of their comfort zone, dealing well with ambiguity and vulnerability. They are self-aware, adapting to make others comfortable, putting others at ease, and creating a sense of relatability and approachability. They step aside to provide opportunities for others to take the stage, and they applaud their accomplishments.

Empathy

Collaborative male leaders show their concern for people. They are demonstratively caring and perceptive while maintaining command of their own emotions. They pay attention to what others are feeling, considering what it's like to "walk in their shoes," and using that understanding as a basis for a functional, positive relationship. They look to improve others' work experiences and help make their lives better.

Listening

Collaborative executive men pay attention to what others are saying, making a concerted effort to listen, to ask, and to check their assumptions. They win over others by showing curiosity and interest, proactively reaching out to others, and soliciting others' opinions first before sharing their own. They watch for nonverbal cues, such as facial expressions and body language, while listening to what is actually being said in order to gain a more complete understanding.

Respecting All

Collaborative male leaders acknowledge others and get to know them, no matter their background or position on the corporate ladder. They go out of their way to engage people at all levels of the organization. They show high regard for all employees and specifically spell out to individuals why their roles are valued and what their contributions are to the organization.

Organizational Leadership

Driving Mission and Meaningfulness

Collaborative executive men embrace their role as steward of the culture, believe strongly in what their organization stands for, and see its social importance. They inspire others to embrace the mission of the organization as a catalyst to unify the workforce. They reinforce the purpose of the organization, giving people a sense of contributing to a greater cause. They are thought leaders, speaking about issues such as diversity, inclusion, and corporate governance. They foster an ethical culture and mentor the next generation of leaders with an eye for improving the culture of their industries.

Cultivating Shared Accountability

Collaborative male leaders cultivate accountability by making it a reciprocal imperative, by sharing goals, and by holding themselves responsible for their people's success. They actively contract with others. They clarify roles and how each person contributes. They fuel others' efforts by expressing confidence that they "*can* do it," and they work alongside them to ensure that they do. They build a network of relationships to stay connected and monitor project progress, creating a process to maintain collaboration and accountability in a collegial way.

Developing Future Leaders

Collaborative male leaders take great pride in developing others. They have a keen eye for emerging talent. With their empathy and listening, they pick up on characteristics and strengths in others that may be missed by their peers. They give people a chance to "take the wheel," and analyze failures and successes. These men take ownership of their own learning and continued development and encourage those who work with them to do the same.

There you have it, the Collaboration Code!

Now, let's sit back and hear from these collaborative men about how they apply the skills of the Men's New Leadership Blueprint to lead culture change and nurture tomorrow's leaders.

CHAPTER 5

Share the Spotlight: Tempering Ego

"More the knowledge, lesser the ego. Lesser the knowledge, more the ego."

–Albert Einstein

In today's team-based business environment, where building trust and engaging employees is essential for success, leaders have to be inclusive, not independently forging ahead for others to follow. That means they need to have empathy and to listen; they need to show respect for people at every level; they need to cultivate shared accountability; and they need to drive meaningfulness and the mission. In order to do this, men need to have their ego under control.

Yet we have a history of business leaders who were bigger than life, looked up to for their independent thinking, steadfastness, and bravado. They were men with big egos and served as examples of what male leaders should be. That illusion is still present. Yet, for many of those leaders, their egocentric styles had a negative effect.

Jack Welch's leadership of GE has been widely lauded, a great deal of that praise from those who did not actually work for him. When I was talking with a former director of the company, he said people on the inside felt they couldn't speak up; they couldn't say no. He continued, "In the corporate world, that desire for the best, brightest, authoritative leader died because of failures brought on by the fact that people under those leaders stayed quiet about what wasn't working. This non-collaborative, egocentric leadership style led to the Enron disasters of the world."

A particularly abrasive example of this ego-full leadership style causing disasters is that of "Chainsaw" Al Dunlap, a man who compared himself to Bruce Springsteen and was known for his slash and burn methodology. As CEO, he gutted Scott Paper to sell it off, then ran Sunbeam into the ground, as reported in the Wall Street Journal, "because of quality problems, management turmoil and disarray in the supply chain."

In direct contrast, the *Good to Great* study by Jim Collins found that leaders who are modest, show personal humility, are self-effacing and understated—not larger-than-life celebrity leaders—attained extraordinary company results as measured by cumulative stock returns over a fifteen-year period. This is a stark difference from two-thirds of the comparison companies in their study that had leaders "with gargantuan personal egos that contributed to the demise or continued mediocrity of the company."[6]

Jim Collins found that leaders who are modest, show personal humility, are self-effacing and understated—not larger-than-life celebrity leaders—attained extraordinary company results

Similarly, I found that today's successful collaborative male leaders temper their ego. They get out of their own way. They show personal humility and vulnerability, not needing to prove themselves or look for affirmation. They listen to others instead of dominating the conversation in order to shore up their position. While they may be chomping at the bit to demonstrate their mastery of subjects and crow about their achievements, they instead pause to provide opportunities for those around them to take the stage. They do not compete for attention.

These men show up as the adult in the room. They do not have temper tantrums, pound their fists on nearby surfaces, or continually talk about how great they are. And when they show up as adults, they create an environment where others can grow, have fun, and be productive. This actually serves to build and maintain their ego. But it is a healthy, balanced ego that they build and maintain, one that gives them an internal sense of well-being and satisfaction, not one that is the toxic egomaniacal variety obsessed with its own sense of greatness.

Male leaders recognize that tempering ego isn't just a nice way of being. Many have told me that if they didn't keep their ego in check, they would fail. Charles, our CEO in educational services, talked about a time early in his career when he let pride get in the way of his own advancement. He wanted to be recognized publicly for his achievements by being promoted to a coveted position opening up in his part of the organization. Rather than going to his boss and making the case for his ascension to that role, he waited for it to be granted to him. He didn't want anyone to have the impression that he lobbied for it and didn't authentically earn it. He said, "I should have stepped up and said, 'I want this job.' But instead, I waited, wanting to be acknowledged as the perfect person for it. I wanted that external affirmation and public recognition. Someone else was promoted instead." He recognized that he should have managed his pride and ego rather than letting it manage him. He should have balanced his assertiveness and confidence with humility.

HUMILITY AND VULNERABILITY

Collaborative male leaders demonstrate a strong self-assuredness that is a blend of confidence and humility. In most situations, that is critical to leading successfully, particularly when working with super egos. Kevin, our senior vice president in a multi-entity healthcare organization, has the "enviable" job of implementing a change that will ultimately streamline the system, organizing it by service lines and surgical services rather than by facilities across the region. Needless to say, this man has his hands full with managing a lot of other egos. Perhaps as a result, there just isn't room for him to supersize his own. He said, "I have to be confident, but not arrogant." He sees his success as tied to what he called "the art of influence," which to him means setting ego aside and not dictating what to do. He knows that it's the only way he can "herd cats." He added, "It's less about my idea; it's our idea together. I don't get recognition, and I can rest comfortably with that. I don't need the recognition."

Interestingly, when I was consulting with a group of physician leaders in another healthcare system, they said they also relied on influence to lead their medical colleagues. They called it "a casual negotiation." They were uncomfortable having a formal hierarchical relationship and instead preferred to think of their role as a representative of their team of physicians to the administration management. The driver of this egalitarian team leadership was wanting to not tread on the egos of other physicians. As physicians themselves, these leaders knew all too well about big egos, and they learned to sidestep their own egos to manage them.

The leaders in both of these examples set their own egos aside and, in doing so, they also tamed the egos of individuals in the team. Their humility set an egalitarian tone that was essential to defuse power struggles and to establish and facilitate collaborative interaction.

Their humility set an egalitarian tone that was essential to defuse power struggles and to establish and facilitate collaborative interaction.

Confidence with a healthy dash of humility enables successful male leaders to eschew an aversion to uncertainty and admit when they are out of their comfort zone and need help. They are able to be vulnerable.

Patrick, our business unit president of a manufacturing giant, talked for fifteen minutes about his humble beginnings. He had a learning disability but never wanted the accommodation of getting extra time on tests. "I was going to get through it the same way everybody else did." But he admitted, "It was hard though. They were trying to weed us out. I thought about picking a different major, but then I got stubborn and just said, 'Man, I'm finishing this.' And so I stuck with electrical engineering."

He reflected that his early experience of struggling to make the grade despite his disability prepared him for being tapped for a quick rise in his company. He was used to shoring up his confidence in order to take on responsibilities he wasn't sure he could perform.

He was twenty-six years old when he was running sales for four states. He said, "I was promoted way beyond my capabilities. I was way out of my comfort zone, but I handled it. I asked for help." Not only did Patrick step into an arena without feeling even 50 percent prepared, he wasn't afraid to admit it to those around him. And he wasn't reluctant to talk to me about it either.

Patrick told me about his promotion from role to role, going state to state. After those moves, he accepted another position that he didn't know if he could pull off. "It was a business that was bankrupt; we had to turn it around. There were a lot of people quitting. I'd go and hire back some people who had left, found some new people, built a team, and we put together a nice strategy." He was quick to add, "I made sure there was clarity around everybody's roles contributing to the greater win."

This was the first of several turnarounds he led. The details were different, but the way he went about it was very much the same. He assembled the team—removing some people, adding others—and then coached them to work collaboratively and worked collaboratively with them. He credits business successes to "we had a great team" and truly believed it was them, not him, who made the difference.

When I met with Patrick, he was gracious, humble, and comfortable in his own skin. We sat at the rectangular table in his office on the same side but facing one another. There was no desk or conference table between us to create a barrier. He presented himself as open and welcoming. He in no way flaunted his expertise, his experience, his senior leadership position. The blend of confidence and humility was evident.

SELF-AWARENESS

I met Andrew, the prominent publishing executive, in his Manhattan office on a sweltering summer day. It turned out that my train was an hour late, Andrew's office was a mile away, and my meeting was supposed to start in two minutes. I headed out on foot, keeping an eye out for an available cab that never appeared. I arrived eighteen minutes late for my meeting, certain that my feet were bleeding and absolutely sure that the back of my head was soaked from perspiration.

When I arrived on the top floor, Andrew was standing there to greet me and wave me on to follow him to his office. His desk faced the far end of the room by the windows, taking advantage of the awesome view, and the side walls were shelved with books. I sat at the far end of his conference table, in front of the window air conditioner. Andrew asked, "Are you okay there? That air is blasting right on you." Actually, it was a relief to feel the icy breeze, but I appreciated Andrew being so kind and concerned about my comfort. He handed me a water from his refrigerator and sat catty-corner to me. I actually forgot about the blistered soles of my feet and my damp hair. He had put me at ease within minutes, and interviewing him was a "breeze."

Being a member of a prominent family, Andrew has been in a position of high status pretty much all of his life. Perhaps that status was further cemented by the risks and achievements he has taken throughout his career. He is keenly aware that his position can intimidate people and counteracts that with a solicitous, warmhearted style. He said to me, "It's my responsibility to take care of people here. I think I'm probably a little more humanistic than most guys who are in my position." From my own experience, I'd say that is most certainly true.

Male leaders who have their ego under control are self-aware, as Andrew demonstrated; they have to be. After all, it is awareness that helps keep them in check. They perceive how others respond to them and adapt to make them comfortable. Given their position at the highest levels in their organizations, these men know that their title and experience can be intimidating. Perhaps, in a way, their awareness of this and their intention to mitigate it actually reinforces their humility. Tom, a self-aware Fortune 50 chief executive and board chair once told me that the failure of many CEOs is that "they start to believe everything written about them." In other words, the accolades go to their head, and it doesn't fit through the door anymore. He also told me that this was the biggest difference he sees in male and female CEOs, saying, "Women don't have a big ego that you have to deal with."

Charles, our CEO in the educational services, when on site, spends half his day working in an open common area to make it easier for people to come talk with him. He said, "I have this office, but more times than not, I'm out there. I'm available. I'm approachable. I'm accountable. I don't walk around with the CEO title pinned on my jacket."

In addition to Andrew, I interviewed many other male leaders with national or international reputations. It was remarkable to me the skill that Andrew and all of these men possessed in making me feel at ease. The offer of coffee, tea, or water was just the beginning of it. They themselves were relaxed, which rubbed off on me. Actually, there was one CEO who seemed a little nervous, explaining that he was not sure if he was giving me the information I needed. Funny, I found myself relax as I was trying to make him feel more comfortable, which worked. My point here is that comfort begets comfort.

Being aware of how you impact others' emotions, and then adjusting to put them at ease, is an important component of keeping your ego in check.

Being aware of how you impact others' emotions, and then adjusting to put them at ease, is an important component of keeping your ego in check. Men who are confident and comfortable in their own skin do this. It immediately tamps down that urge to impress and establish status. It also arrests that urge in others around them. And it's a quality that engages people, makes them feel that they are important, and earns their trust. It creates what Harvard Business School professor Amy Edmondson labeled as psychological safety,[7] a critical factor for organizational performance.

TEMPERED EGO DOES NOT MEAN EGO-LESS

Tempering ego does not mean abandoning ego. Daniel, the CEO of a national managed care services provider, put it this way, "I think I have a strong ego, not a big ego. Having a strong ego is necessary to compete, but I keep it in check." Interestingly, he said that he found balance because internally, he struggles with perfection and is competing against himself, so the external acknowledgment doesn't go to his head; his head is busy doing critical self-evaluation. He also made the point that his ego is fed by *setting* the tone of his company's work environment rather than *accepting* the tone, which would be the case if he were not leading the organization.

My research with successful C-suite level women shows that they also don't compete against others but tend to compete against their own best performance. By not competing with their colleagues, they avoid posing as a rival rather than teammate. Perhaps what these women did can provide an example to their male counterparts. The secret of tempering ego for men may be to shift

> *The secret of tempering ego for men may be to shift their focus away from "the competition" and onto their own high expectations of themselves.*

their focus away from "the competition" and onto their own high expectations of themselves.

BUILDING AND MAINTAINING A TEMPERED EGO

The men I interviewed have various ways of building and maintaining a tempered ego. Several of them do this through activities and achievements outside the office. For example, Stephen, our CEO of a human services organization who runs the organization collaboratively with his CAO and COO, told me he maintains his ego by extolling the success of his organization. "I feed my ego by presenting around the world about what we have achieved and learned. I share our experience as a model for other countries." Then he said to me, "I give a lot of credit to Bill and Rachel (COO and CAO)." Yes, he shares credit with the other leaders, but he loves being out there telling their story in front of large audiences, because it is *his* story; he invented the model; he built the organization. He actually seemed to light up when talking with me about it.

Dane, our senior VP in technology and communications, told me that his competitiveness comes out in mastering things that are unrelated to work. He became interested in an art form called Encaustic Giclée where one applies wax on top of a print to create texture. He learned it and continues to perfect it. "I've learned to channel my energy this way, diffuse it in other areas." He added, "I compete on tasks, not with people. I've learned you piss people off when you compete with them."

Not all, but many of the executive men I interviewed were noticeably very fit. I would chuckle to myself when I encountered yet another guy who clearly worked out and was the picture of masculinity. Not one of them talked about it, but I couldn't help but think to myself these men present themselves as strongly masculine and self-assured, so perhaps their very secure male ego has little problem demonstrating the "feminine characteristics" of nurturing and inclusiveness. These men have the confidence to use their "soft skills" in leadership.

When I discussed this with Towson University's Andrew Reiner, who is doing research on the future of masculinity,[8] he confirmed that men, particularly younger men, work out and are very focused on presenting themselves in a masculine way. He noted that how they look is very much a part of their identity. "They get their 'man card' stamped by working out; it's how they have a foot in the door on masculinity." In other words, it allows them more freedom to stray from other norms of masculinity and be more balanced.

Creating a Nurturing Environment

In addition to competing against themselves and reaching toward "perfection"—through both physical and professional achievement—men build and maintain their tempered egos by nurturing others, creating an environment where others can grow, and thereby feel needed.

Charles, who turned around a struggling educational services organization, told me about giving his executive assistant, Lorraine, the opportunity to present at a board meeting. He said, "We were getting ready for strategic planning, so I was reading *Blue Ocean Strategy* [a book about creating lasting success by discovering and targeting untapped new market spaces]. I was going to open the board meeting with a presentation about the book."

When Charles saw that Lorraine had bought a copy of the book and was reading it "along with him," he decided to ask her to do the presentation. He explained to me that he would have loved to present the material; it was impressive stuff, and it would make him look good, but it was a great opportunity for his assistant to shine, so he kept his ego in check. He said, "I would love to tell you this, like I'm a pious guy, but I'm human and have to work on it."

He admitted it required a concerted effort to temper his ego; it wasn't easy for him. He said he fights his ego all the time. "I own the fact that it exists. I constantly think about it. But the fight pays off." Although giving Lorraine visibility meant stepping out of the spotlight himself, it was worth it to him. What he got from it was an ego boost, taking pride in Lorraine's successful presentation to the board.

For others, tempering ego by nurturing others seems to come naturally. Nick, the general counsel of a public transportation company, takes pride in the accomplishments of people reporting to him, more so than his own achievements. "I get a lot of satisfaction watching others rise to the occasion and knowing that my encouragement and leadership was a catalyst for that. I usually map out the road to a solution of a complicated problem—who needs to be involved, what message should the solution send, who or what will get in the way, and how can I minimize that." Then he keeps this map in his back pocket unless he needs to jump in to help.

He lets his direct reports run with their own plan, staying in the background to assist if necessary. He doesn't feel the need to demonstrate his skills. In fact, doing that and getting acknowledgment and pats on the back isn't what feeds his ego. Rather, "I get a big kick when the solution unfolds largely as I envisioned but as the result of a collaborative effort and not my preaching."

Seeing others succeed and grow as a source of accomplishment was a theme throughout my interviews with executive men. Their feeling of accomplishment was about helping others succeed rather than about their own achievements. It was a boost to their egos. I had to dig a bit to find this ego piece underlying all this nurturing-people-and-letting-them-shine philosophy. I found out that it wasn't simply a matter of altruism; it was an ego boost. For some of the men I talked with, this was a discovery for them as well, brought about by our conversations.

Successful executive men take pride in creating an atmosphere that allows their people to excel. They take further pride from that atmosphere being a competitive advantage. It builds their ego. Vincent, who heads up global capital markets in a large financial institution, deliberately creates an environment for his people to thrive, one where they feel that they are relevant, that they can make a difference and can have fun. He takes pride in the fact that he has created a better culture than his competitors in the industry.

He said one mid-level professional told him that her husband noticed a difference in her since she started working there, having left another company several months before. He said that now she was happy. Vincent told me, "When people come to our organization and after a few weeks on the job, they go home and their spouse says, 'You're a different person, a happier person and a better person,' then I feel a real sense of achievement."

Vincent believes it is the atmosphere he provides that allows people to do their best work. "They're good people, happy people, because we have an environment where our good comes out." He added, "Clearly outside of here, in the industry, it's a whole different atmosphere."

But hold on, Vincent has an interesting twist to this "creating-a-nurturing-culture-and-taking-pride-in-his-people-thriving-because-of-it" narrative. Later in the course of our discussion, I asked him directly, "Are you competitive?" He said "Yes; as we have expanded, I have lifted whole teams from our competitors." Couldn't help but notice a little twinkle of delight in his eyes. I could see that Vincent's ego was definitely stoked by beating out the competition.

For Paul, the CEO of a nonprofit behavioral health and educational services organization, it's a matter of creating a nurturing environment because "it feels good to him when colleagues feel a part of the achievement. It's more fun when we are working together." He said, "I get a personal sense of satisfaction when my colleagues at every level of the organization feel invested in a way that I do." That's one way he maintains a strong ego. Another is by achieving the organization's goals; that is, through his leadership, they are delivering high quality service and hitting the financial metrics both he and the board expect.

About achieving goals, he said, "It ties in with my own ambition. I mean, I wouldn't have worked toward achieving a CEO position from being a social worker if I didn't have that. I pursued that. I like being in charge. And running a big complex organization is just wicked fun for me. And it's really fun when we kind of all do this together. My leadership is a part of bringing people together."

Filling a Need

Being sought out to provide guidance, advice, and support is flattering. Men who temper ego do not let that go to their head. Instead, they let the affirmation soak in and energize them.

Kevin said he feels valued by being needed. "I ask myself, 'Am I moving the dial, getting results?' But success is more than EBITDA [earnings before interest, taxes, depreciation, and amortization]. I feel powerful when I am making a difference to young people here." He said, "Soon after I got here, I had a conversation with my team. I sat rather than stood to talk. I told my story about being a therapist, how I got to this role. I gave them contact numbers and my expectations and told them, 'I'm here to move barriers.' After my talk, three people came up and wanted to talk about their careers. They were looking to me for advice. That is rewarding. The need to feel needed, you feel fulfilled."

Many male leaders I interviewed spoke with pride about being an industry expert sought out to share their experience. Although some of the satisfaction was surely in being lauded on the podium, the impression I got was that they also felt honored that they could provide guidance. Similarly, several chief executives expressed great satisfaction in mentoring others, in feeling needed to impart their learning and experience to a less experienced CEO or upcoming executive.

Tempering ego is a foundational competency in many ways. It paves the way for other critical characteristics such as empathy, listening, and respecting all, which are crucial to relationship building, establishing trust, and developing others. It also allows for humility, a comfort with showing vulnerability, and self-awareness, all of which make leaders more approachable. Without tempering their ego, leaders cannot see beyond themselves to connect and relate to others.

Men temper their ego in a variety of ways. Interestingly, they also build and maintain their egos through the very same actions. They show humility and dare to be vulnerable. They are self-aware and adjust how they present themselves and interact with others in order to put them at ease. They are comfortable in their own skin. It is that inner contentment with themselves and their accomplishments, rather than relying on external sources of recognition, that shores up their confidence and allows them to show humility.

They focus their competitiveness on beating their own best rather than beating out others. They gain great satisfaction and a sense of pride from nurturing others, individually and through creating a supportive work environment, and helping them grow professionally. Men who temper their ego are more relatable, enhance their credibility, and increase their ability to influence and connect with others. It makes them approachable. It shows they care about what others have to say. It helps build trusting relationships. In short, these traits make people want to work with them. These are critical traits for leading collaboratively and, ultimately, for being a more successful leader.

Men who temper their ego are more relatable, enhance their credibility, and increase their ability to influence and connect with others.

CHAPTER 6

Dare to Care: Empathy, Listening, and Respecting All

"People will forget what you said, people will forget what you did, but people will never forget how you made them feel."

–Maya Angelou

Empathy, listening, and respecting all are characteristics that communicate to others, "I care," "I'm interested," and "I understand." These traits engender connections and solidify teams. Empathy is essential for leading highly diverse, multi-generational teams. It builds trust and effective relationships. Research by Daniel Goleman and other researchers has shown a correlation between empathy and effectively leading teams.[9] Consequently, academics and consultants have scurried to define empathy and how you can develop it in yourself. But can you develop empathy? Well, if you care and you pay attention, yes you can. That means that you respect others, no matter their role and status in the company, and you listen to them.

Empathy, simply stated, is being aware of what others are feeling, considering what it's like to "walk in their shoes," and using that understanding as a basis for a functional, positive relationship. Collaborative leaders acknowledge others and get to know them. They go out of their way to engage people at all levels of the organization. They pay attention to what others are saying, making a concerted effort to listen to them, to ask them questions, and to check assumptions. These are the leaders who say hello to the janitor, maintenance staff, and clerk. You've probably heard if you want to get a good sense of someone's character, witness how they treat a restaurant server. It's appalling—and revealing—how so many people will not notice, will merely ignore, or will be downright rude to those they see as beneath them.

THREE FACETS OF EMPATHY

Jamil Zaki, in his book *The War for Kindness: Building Empathy in a Fractured World*,[10] explains that empathy is really "an umbrella term that describes multiple ways people respond to one another." He defines three types of empathy:

- Cognitive Empathy: explicitly considering someone else's point of view

- Emotional Empathy: sharing the feelings that another is experiencing

- Empathetic Concern: wishing to improve someone else's experience or well-being

Each of these aspects of empathy showed up in my research with collaborative male leaders.

Cognitive Empathy

A somewhat universal capability that I've found in collaborative leaders is cognitive empathy. They want to know how others are experiencing their job and the organization, and proactively venture out of their offices to find out. They look to others as they make decisions, thinking about how they would feel, and indeed, talking with them to hear firsthand about their point of view. They have an egalitarian mindset, truly not thinking of themselves as superior to anyone else.

Kevin told me, "I have a philosophy in life, which is to appreciate what people bring to every part of the organization and to make sure that they understand that we not only acknowledge and recognize it, but value it." Earlier in his career, Kevin had seen senior level people disregard others, and it bothered him. "I saw C-suite executives that would come out and they would never acknowledge people; they only wanted to go out to be visible and to be seen by and be associated with the top people. And so, as they walked down the hall, they wouldn't look at you in the eye. They wouldn't even say hello. Why would you not pause and just introduce yourself or at a minimum say, 'I appreciate what you do?'"

So perhaps that early experience fueled Kevin to take deliberate action as a new executive in his organization and demonstrate his respect for all employees. He said, "I walked down to the basement my first day in my role as the operations officer. The ladies down there, many of them have worked here for decades folding our linen every day, they're listening to their gospel music and laughing. They make minimum wage. I pulled a chair up, took my jacket and tie off, and sat down with them for thirty minutes. I wanted to know who they were, why they got up every day. One lady took four buses to get to her job. She told me, 'I've worked here for thirty-two years, and I've never had a leader at the executive rank come out of the office and sit down and talk to us.' And I said, 'Well, let me tell you why I am. Do you realize we couldn't take care of patients if you didn't do your job? Can you imagine taking care of patients without clean sheets on the beds? Not having the fresh towels in the operating room?'"

Kevin was on a roll, telling me about his campaign to make the employees who were often not recognized feel appreciated. He continued, "Then I went to the supply room to see the people who were unloading boxes. They're also not used to seeing the C-suite executives walk through their space. And I ask, 'What is it like here from your perspective?' I feel a humbleness and a deep appreciation for all of the people in the organization and what they do to help us take care of others."

Kevin's egalitarian mindset and cognitive empathy drove him to proactively connect with the hourly workers who keep things running smoothly behind the scenes and to spend time with them to understand their point of view.

Nick also showed cognitive empathy but with a different spin. He makes a point of regularly introducing himself, asking others their names and where they work, often when riding the elevator up to his office. But different from Kevin, who was on a mission to connect and express appreciation for those on lower rungs of the organization, Nick's quest was to connect with everyone he encountered and humanize their perception of the company's executives. Although hundreds of people work in his headquarters building, he tries to remember as many names as he can. As one of the guys in the top floor executive suite, he knows—showing his cognitive empathy—that people can feel uncomfortable with them. He deliberately looks to put people at ease and "put a human face on" the image of top management.

Nick—as well as other collaborative male leaders I've interviewed—believes that by reaching out and trying to get to know people, he is creating a culture that is more engaging, where people feel they matter and are a significant part of the team, much like Vincent, who heads up global capital markets in a large financial institution.

Vincent is a self-described introvert, but he makes a point of connecting with people at all levels. He keeps track of who he hasn't talk with in a while—literally makes a list of who he needs to reach out to that week every Monday morning—to make sure he grabs coffee, has lunch, or checks in with people throughout the company on a regular basis. Vincent sees his efforts to reach out as prompting others to do the same, thereby creating an environment where ready communication up, down, and across the organization and with clients makes them a top performer in the industry.

Emotional Empathy

Collaborative male leaders I've interviewed and have worked with are able to show emotional empathy. I say "able to" because some men consciously or subconsciously suppress those reactions, because "feeling the pain" or the joy of another person makes them vulnerable. This is the kind of empathy that is perhaps the most difficult to manage as you try to stay composed in a business setting. The joy isn't a problem; it's the pain you feel that can be tough to bear. The adrenaline boost of high fives and fist pumps over another's achievement is wonderful. But telling someone you like that they are being let go, seeing the look on their face, and feeling the compassionate lump in your throat is awful. And it's probably more difficult when you try to hide it. But it is the part of empathy that conveys that "you get it," that you really do recognize what someone is feeling.

Some executive men have admitted that they are emotional, that they feel the emotions of others all too well. The difficulty is controlling their own reaction. Brené Brown, in her book *Dare to Lead*,[11] makes the point that it's important to maintain boundaries. She quips, "If struggle is being down a hole, empathy is not jumping into the hole with someone who is struggling and taking on their emotions or owning their struggle as yours to fix. If their issues become yours, now you have two people stuck in a hole."

> *It's critical for your effectiveness as a leader and for your well-being to successfully navigate that space between sharing another's pain and internalizing it.*

It's critical for your effectiveness as a leader and for your well-being to successfully navigate that space between sharing another's pain and internalizing it. I can relate to the struggle executive men have controlling their emotional reactions. As a psychologist and consultant, I constantly have to monitor my emotional reactions to my clients. Early in my career, a colleague said, "You are a sponge. You absorb all the bad feelings people have, and it drags you down. You've got to stop doing that to yourself." To this day I think of him when I feel myself starting to go down into that hole Brené talks about, and I push myself back up.

One of the most in-depth conversations I had about emotional empathy was with Rafael, our CEO of a biological services organization. He thinks he differs from other male leaders he has worked with because he tends to wear his emotions on his sleeve. He said, "If I'm in a situation where somebody is going through something difficult, or we're talking about a difficult topic, or we're celebrating something, I tend to not guard myself from expressing those emotions. I feel them and I show them." He reflected on other men in his role, saying, "I think some leaders do guard themselves because they feel like they need to be this pragmatic, all-knowing, non-vulnerable guy."

Rafael thinks his ability to emotionally connect is an important part of being a leader, but he acknowledges that it doesn't work for everybody. He said, "Expressing emotions and being comfortable when somebody else is expressing emotions is not an easy thing. Some of my colleagues and predecessors and people that I've interacted with have a hard time with that."

Rafael took the concept of emotional empathy as a means of connection further. He talked about his empathy creating a work environment where people can openly be themselves, working with more fervor. In other words, empathy impacts the bottom line by allowing people to fully express themselves. "At the end of the day, you're asking people to do extraordinary things for you. They're going to feel emotions while they're doing that, right? And if you deny them the opportunity to be able to express those emotions or see those emotions in you, then I don't think we reach our full potential."

Patrick, unlike Rafael, was perpetually in a position of being a new leader and establishing himself with a new team. He talked about his turnaround challenges where he had to firmly guide his team to up their game. In one situation, he knew people were not used to performing at a high level. Deadlines were more like guidelines to them. He knew people would be very uncomfortable as he pushed the accelerator. He said, "I had a forecast discussion with my team, and it was a tough love meeting around a few things. The hard part is, I leave there, and I feel bad because they're all going to go home and kick the trashcan over."

He shared that he went home after those meetings and felt like he wanted to kick over a trashcan too. He felt their frustration. He said, "I wanted to make sure they understood the empathy I had about their frustration, and that I do care about them and I believe they can do it." The team's performance improved dramatically, meeting the ambitious goals Patrick had set with them for the survival of their business unit. Patrick thought his emotional empathy for the people on that team was a factor in their success. His team caught on that he was feeling what they were feeling. Even though he was trying to stay positive and focus on his belief that they could do it, he had to meet his team "where they were" and take in how they were feeling too.

Empathetic Concern

Collaborative leaders are motivated to improve others' experiences, to have a major impact on the lives and careers of the people in their charge. They are driven to nurture talented individuals, providing them with opportunities to grow and advance. Later, we will talk specifically about executives' shared drive to develop leaders. The collaborative men in this study also generally showed concern for others at all levels of their companies, wanting to make their lives better.

Remember Kevin, who visited the women folding linens in the basement of one of their hospitals? He increased their compensation, adding a component that recognized patient satisfaction for the appearance of the facilities. He said, "I wanted to help them out. Every little bit counts."

Let's also go back to Nick, who uses his elevator rides to introduce himself and learn people's names. He also talks with people to learn more about them and how things are going for them at work. Nick knew from conversations with the legal secretaries that they were concerned by their lack of advancement opportunities in the company. He felt their frustration, and it stirred his own past experiences of wanting to take on more responsibilities but not having the latitude to do so.

Nick's empathetic concern drove him to change policy. "One of our paralegals retired, and I decided to open up that position to legal secretaries. There are no other jobs for them here. Paralegals are a trained professional job, but a legal secretary really has the same skill set. So I went out on a limb and did this."

Since the legal secretaries who applied for paralegal positions needed to obtain the paralegal qualification in one year, he agreed to sponsor them, paying the fees for them to get the certificate. "There's probably a ten percent pay difference, which is a game changer for a person who's living paycheck to paycheck. It changes their life, so it's very exciting to me to offer them that opportunity." Nick's job satisfaction and measure of his performance as a leader is driven by acting on his empathetic concern.

TOOLS OF EMPATHY

When I asked collaborative executive men what characteristics are most important for a leader, listening was the one they most commonly cited. They are not alone; Harvard Business Review has a thousand case studies and hundreds of articles related to leadership and listening in their library. The other characteristic executives talked about extensively was respecting people. It doesn't surprise me that these two characteristics topped the list of important traits since you can only have empathy for others if you care and listen to them.

Listening with Your Ears, Eyes, and Heart

Our healthcare system CEO, Neil, associates listening with continuous learning, not thinking you know everything by the time you get the corner office; he maintains curiosity. He said, "We've all been told for years that listening is important. I think it's one of the most important characteristics of a leader. I just met with another CEO yesterday who talked about how critical listening was and reflected on how he had changed over his career as a result. I don't think you can be learning and growing and becoming better if you don't listen. But it's a hard skill when you're in charge."

> *"I don't think you can be learning and growing and becoming better if you don't listen. But it's a hard skill when you're in charge."*

Part of the conversation between Neil and the other CEO was about what can get in the way of listening. Neil said, "Over the course of your career, it's about getting rid of the ego and the need to prove your knowledge. Right?" Yes, right. To have empathy, you need to be curious and you need to listen, which means you need to stop taking airtime to prove yourself.

The most common meaning of listening is paying attention to what is being said. While this can include listening to everything from a live presentation to a podcast, the executive men I spoke with focused on personal interactions, listening to another individual in a conversation or meeting. For some leaders, this means switching off their mental process of formulating a response to what is being said, since devising a response means you miss the entirety of the message being conveyed. For others, it means not giving in to the urge to exhibit expertise and prove themselves, as Neil and his CEO friend discussed. Essentially, listening well only happens when the listener isn't distracted by his own thoughts. You must focus outward, not inward.

I learned this concept from my son when he was a rather articulate six-year-old. His teacher had separated him from his best friend, seating them on opposite sides of the classroom because she thought they were distracting each other and not listening. My son explained to me that it wasn't his friend who was distracting him, rather, "I get distracted by my own thoughts." That answer blew me away because it was so perceptive and on point. And in the intervening fifteen years, he has learned to tame his ever-active thought centers and deliberately attend to listening.

Collaborative executives mentioned that they not only listened to people's words, but also paid attention to body language as a way to really understand what the other person was feeling. They thought they could be more effective listeners if they used their eyes as well as their ears. Body language and facial expressions add nuance to what is being said, and therefore, allow you to collect much more data. Watching non-verbal cues while listening to what is actually being said gives a more complete picture.

Charles described how reading body language clues in one particular meeting allowed him to have a very different, more accurate view of people's perceptions. "Everyone left that meeting thinking everything went well because everyone said all the right things. I had to correct them. 'No, I'm not feeling this was a positive meeting.' People were fidgeting, distracted by noises outside the room, not making eye contact. I believe I'm very tuned in that way. Really listening, really being fully present, paying attention. I watch and I see. I pick up on things. It's allowed me to go with my instinct a lot."

Nick also stressed the importance of listening and reading body language. He said, "Lawyers like to talk, right? But if you actually listen to what the witness is saying, and you kind of read their body language or the jury's or the judge's, that really lets you know what people are thinking and feeling."

Nick said, "I can tell when somebody's actually listening to me, and I'm sure they can tell if I'm actually listening to them. And I think it's part of that care thing. I care enough to listen to what they have to say, or they care enough to listen to what I have to say."

You can see why empathy and listening are so closely associated. When you listen, you indeed show you care and that you're conveying emotional empathy. And without listening with both your ears and eyes, you won't see the emotions of others. Think about how hard it can be to correctly decipher the feelings in an email or a text (without emoji). There is no opportunity for real empathy. You are working in a vacuum without the emotional cues that you get from hearing or seeing. Instead, in that void, the emotion you may read into the words is really coming from within yourself.

Proactive listening includes being available and actively soliciting others to share how they are feeling. Kevin used his ability to listen and convey emotional empathy as he worked to consolidate obstetrics services while managing his own emotional reactions. Working with the physician leaders and hospital presidents was no walk in the park, as you can imagine. How did he do it? He told me, "I said to them, 'So let's look at the facts first.' But then I realized I had to let them express their feelings. I mean, you can't just suppress those, right? You have to allow them to be out there, and you have to recognize them. So I called them out. I pivoted from the facts and said, 'Okay, look, you brought five doctors here with you thinking you're going to be delivering babies here forever, that's going to be tough to change those expectations. So let's talk through that.'" Kevin helped the physicians clarify their feelings. In clarifying them, they could more readily deal with those feelings rationally. But also, Kevin realized that while communicating facts is important, for a leader to inspire and influence others, a leader must also connect emotionally.

> *While communicating facts is important, for a leader to inspire and influence others, a leader must also connect emotionally.*

Kevin knew it was going to be an emotionally charged situation. And he was empathetic. He'd gone through a similar process at a previous health system. The challenge was not to let his emotional empathy trigger an uncontained response in him. He said, "I have to try to keep my emotions in check. I remind myself I have to remain emotionally intelligent, or I will render myself ineffective." He also was quite aware that if he didn't keep his own emotions in check, he would not be able to hear and understand the doctors' specific concerns.

Soliciting feedback to gain a better understanding of others' emotions and showing emotional empathy are essential parts of persuasion, as Kevin so adeptly demonstrated as he successfully got physician leaders and hospital presidents on board with consolidating obstetrics across the system. Sharing the emotion of the situation allowed Kevin and the team to reach a decision that all parties felt was the right one.

Respecting All

At the beginning of this chapter, we saw that an enabler of cognitive empathy is respecting all people, caring enough to chat with them and listen to their experiences. It is an egalitarian mindset that recognizes that we are no better or no worse than anyone else. Kevin respected the housekeepers and supply room workers. Nick demonstrated his respect by learning people's names.

For Charles, whose listening includes reading body language, respect is about being demonstrative and not patronizing. He said, "It's about getting out of your shell if you are shy by nature." He also explained the important benefits of respect. "I think wisdom comes from a lot of places. I don't believe that just because I have some lofty title that I have the answer to everything. So, I honor the exchange, I respect the exchange with people."

"I think wisdom comes from a lot of places. I don't believe that just because I have some lofty title that I have the answer to everything."

Vincent, the guy who makes a list every Monday of who he should reach out to that week, thinks vulnerability and humility are crucial leadership traits. He says, "The humility part goes back to treating everyone with respect. People that are humble treat people with respect."

Interestingly, Vincent also tied the idea of respecting all to establishing and maintaining a high-quality reputation. "When I talk to the new kids, the management development professionals, I try to encourage them to treat every conversation as an important conversation because you're building your brand within the organization. Whether you're talking to the janitor or our CEO, those conversations are discussed. That janitor may say to someone, 'Hey, that person was nice enough to have a conversation with me.' You have that conversation with the janitor because it's the right thing to do, but it's also about building your brand, being known as open, down-to-earth, compassionate. That brand is important when you are being considered for job opportunities."

DEVELOPING EMPATHY

Caring, listening, paying attention, respecting others—they sound like simple tasks, but is that true for everyone? Maybe not.

Daniel, our CEO of a managed care services provider told me, "I'm an introvert, and I realized early on in my role as CEO that I wasn't going to be that model charismatic leader." He is a reserved guy, not demonstratively warm, self-described as "shy," and I can't imagine that he seeks out people at lower levels of his organization like Nick or Kevin do. These tasks would not be simple for him. But his quiet nature didn't strike me as aloof or arrogant. In my time with him, he was friendly and always acknowledged, if not greeted, people in the hallway as we walked to the central conference room. He, like many of us, could push himself out of his comfort zone to be a bit more like Nick or Kevin.

Helen Riess, MD, in her fascinating pragmatic book, *The Empathy Effect: Seven Neuroscience-Based Keys for Transforming the Way We Live, Love, Work, and Connect Across Differences*, presents the case that our capacity for empathy is not just an innate trait, it is also a skill that we can learn and expand.[12] She developed a model and training curriculum, initially for physicians, to recognize and promote empathic behavior in oneself and others.

Of course, there is a whole body of research and many books about emotional intelligence in leadership, which includes paying attention to nonverbals and to how you are responding emotionally to others. Check out Annie McKee's books, *Primal Leadership*[13] and *Resonant Leadership*,[14] for more on this. These empathy skills are all muscles that can be developed, but you have to work out. And to a certain extent, "no pain, no gain" applies here.

> *These empathy skills are all muscles that can be developed, but you have to work out.*

That brings me to the heart of the issue. Men tend to avoid facing emotion, particularly at work, and particularly their own emotional response to others. Being open to others' emotions and letting that trigger themselves to react emotionally—emotional empathy—can make them feel vulnerable. I think many are just afraid of it since they feel out of control. I get it. Remember, I'm the one whose colleague told me to quit being a "sponge." I course corrected a bit too much for a while and suppressed my emotional responses. I felt more in control, but I sacrificed my strength of connecting with people.

As I mentioned earlier, emotional empathy requires carefully maintaining boundaries and, as Brené Brown cautions, "not jumping into the hole with someone who is struggling and taking on their emotions." Helen Riess incorporates self-regulation and self-management techniques in her training, because managing and tamping excessive emotional responses is

Managing and tamping excessive emotional responses is a huge component in being able to handle emotional empathy.

a huge component in being able to handle emotional empathy. Perhaps it was the issue of maintaining boundaries that in the immediate aftermath of #MeToo had led some men to tell me they felt like they couldn't "be human," that they had to act like a robot; they had to be devoid of feeling. These are probably the same men who avoid dealing with emotions so as to maintain control of their own.

Collaborative male leaders have overcome their reluctance to face emotion, if they had any reluctance at all. Certainly, they've gotten very smart about how to regulate their emotional responses. These men consider others' point of view and share feelings others are experiencing. I cannot help but think about the Volcano Men who had to face the powerful emotions of the people displaced by the lava. Those three men could not avoid it. Their success in providing support to evacuees depended on their ability to face emotions, be empathetic, and control their own emotions. Their empathy bonded them with the community.

Rafael, who described himself as naturally emotional, still worries a bit about being vulnerable to manipulation. He said, "We have to deal with the emotions and whatever that person is going through. But if someone is expressing them as a form of manipulation, then my guard goes up." But he offered these words of insight, "I think you need to practice being able to judge that, and the only way you do that is if you leave yourself open to observing that dynamic, as opposed to every time somebody gets emotional, denying yourself the opportunity to show your emotions and hear the emotions of others."

□□□

Collaborative male leaders are demonstratively caring and perceptive while maintaining command of their own emotions. They are curious and use empathy and listening to engender connections, solidify teams, and win over others. They show their interest in understanding the thoughts and feelings of everyone around them, expressing their respect.

CHAPTER 7

Position the Purpose: Driving Mission and Meaningfulness

"A vision is not just a picture of what could be; it is an appeal to our better selves, a call to be something more."

–Rosabeth Moss Kanter

As we saw from the story about the Hub, a strong sense of mission and meaningfulness can unify and bond a group of diverse people and guide them through the uncertainty of change. As such, it is an essential tool for a collaborative leader. Collaborative leaders strongly believe in what their organization stands for and recognize its social importance. They generate a shared sense of purpose, creating a sense of "we" where people feel they are contributing to a greater cause. In doing so, they drive the mission and create a robust culture.

REINFORCING SHARED PURPOSE

Purpose provides a North Star that directs people beyond their own interests and beyond the financial success of the firm. Rather than being tied to a CEO's ideas, his own grandeur, or his ego, the organization is centered on a common intent or mission. It means that leaders at all levels in the organization subdue their own egos to serve that mission. They have a strong sense of personal purpose that is aligned with that of the organization.

Emmet believes his organization exists to better people's lives. He told me, "The experiences that we create for individual human beings is so far above and beyond customer service. We meet people in their life journey, wherever they are, regardless of circumstances and then help them improve their lives. That's who we are as an organization." He explained that he brought all thirteen thousand team members to an off-site at a local convention center to talk about how the organization's "brand promise" needs to actually be the brand experience consistently, no matter what door or avenue their customers come through. "It's my jet fuel. It lights the fire of our team to connect us back to our real purpose and real meaning, which is why many of us decided to get into this industry, but specifically, to join this company."

Stephen, our CEO in human services whose organization coordinates organ transplants between recipients and donors, talked about finding the right people and being a role model for them. "People have to have the mission orientation because it requires a 24/7 commitment. Your personal life is interrupted constantly." Then he reflected, "I stayed on call for many, many years before becoming the CEO." Stephen's dedication to always being available, even now as the CEO, reinforces the organization's purpose. He walks the talk. His whole organization sees that devotion and emulates it. They know that they are in business to make life-changing tragedies more bearable for people and to have a positive outcome, and those heartbreaking events don't follow a schedule.

But what about companies that are not dealing with life and death situations? What is the passionate purpose that a leader can use to unify their organization around a common cause?

John Sargent, CEO of Macmillan Publishers, defended freedom of speech in the face of President Trump's cease and desist order demanding Macmillan stop publication of Michael Wolff's incendiary *Fire and Fury*.[15] John used the moment to put that sense of purpose front and center inside the company, sending a letter to employees rather than writing an op-ed. He wanted it to be a more personal communication to reinforce the company's purpose. He said, "It makes sure all the employees know that this is something that they are standing up for as well. They're Macmillan."

Simon Sinek, the TED talk sensation who told leaders to start with "why" to inspire action, uses the example of Apple to make his point about the importance of purpose. Apple's "why" is to challenge the status quo and empower the individual, which evokes a passion among its employees and customers.

Sinek explains that the reason "why" is so powerful is that it appeals to the limbic part of the brain, the region where feelings and reactions reside. He reasons that when leaders share the "why," people connect to the values and feel a sense of tribal affiliation.[16]

Disney's "why" is to bring happiness to others, so its leaders unify employees around the rallying cry, "Whatever you do is contributing to creating happiness for others."

Kevin, our housekeeping-visiting senior VP, used the "why" to make employees feel like an important part of the organization. He reminded the laundry workers that their mission is to take excellent care of patients and that they couldn't do that without clean linens and beautiful facilities. They were contributing to providing excellent care for their patients.

Vincent reinforces the company's purpose of "working with people and having their backs." He points out that several young professionals who had left the company came back because, unlike other financial institutions, "they felt they were making a meaningful contribution," helping their clients and their coworkers to be successful.

A *Harvard Business Review* article, "Put Purpose at the Core of Your Strategy,"[17] highlights that "many high-growth companies use purpose to generate sustained profitable growth, stay relevant in a rapidly changing world, and deepen ties with their stakeholders." So, in addition to unifying people inside their company and engaging external interest and support, purpose has a strategic role for companies. It allows them to "redefine their playing field," and, therefore, expand *what* they do and/or *how* they do it.

Think of the example of Disney; in focusing on their purpose of bringing happiness to others, they redefined what their company provides and how they provide it. They expanded from films to parks to resorts and more. For example, Disney Institute works with executives to create a culture in their organization that nurtures employee satisfaction and service excellence. In other words, they bring happiness to the company and their stakeholders.

PURPOSE MAKES CHANGE POSSIBLE

Just as companies are able to grow and change when enabled by purpose at the core of their strategy, employees are able to grow and change when they understand purpose. Appreciating the whys, people in the organization can get on board with new directions. It makes for a more flexible, adaptable workforce. It follows that creating a shared sense of purpose is a core competency of collaborative male leaders since it allows people to have a more active and meaningful role in the process. Because they are aligned in a sense of shared purpose, they can productively engage in collective problem solving and decision making, thus, increasing their feeling of having control rather than being powerless. We saw this play out in the case of the Hub where Ikaika's collaborative, inclusive leadership and laser focus on shared purpose grounded evacuees and enabled them to help themselves and each other navigate change.

> *Appreciating the whys, people in the organization can get on board with new directions. It makes for a more flexible, adaptable workforce.*

Patrick was masterful in collaboratively leading people through change. He was involved in several turnarounds, assembling collaborative teams where he kept the business unit purpose—to provide high-end power solutions economically—front and center as they worked together to meet aggressive objectives. Vincent also kept purpose front and center to lead his organization through being acquired by a larger company. He said, "We are the fastest growing provider in the country. We've gotten momentum, but we will lose it if we lose our culture." "We know how to work with people and have their back" is a personal, collaborative purpose that he knew he had to continue to reinforce, particularly through the company's acquisition.

STORYTELLING

How does purpose get woven into the culture? John Coleman, in his book *Passion & Purpose*,[18] writes that purpose is stimulated and reinforced through narrative. Stories make the fabric of culture resilient. It goes beyond corporate legends told and retold within the organization. It is narratives from leaders about how they connect with the company's purpose.

Personal stories about personal motivations, inspire and connect people to the organization's purpose.

Collaborative male leaders, through their personal stories about personal motivations, inspire and connect people to the organization's purpose. Storytelling is a highly effective way to persuade others, and as such, is a prized skill for leaders.

Steve Jobs, storyteller in chief, was legendary for his ability to connect to Apple's purpose and emotionally impact his audience. Jobs shared many personal vignettes that spoke to what Apple was about, including his experience of working with his mechanic father whose penchant for precision and neatness in his garage workshop inspired his own obsession with perfection. On a different emotional level, Howard Schultz, chairman of Starbucks, tells his story about a long-ago trip to Milan and the passion he developed there for the fresh, rich brewed espresso he had discovered and wanted to replicate. It's a story that underscores Starbucks' purpose of providing a satisfying and dependable experience for customers.

A much more personal connection and story comes from an executive I talked with, Miles Wilson, CEO of Education-Works, an organization providing experiential, educational afterschool programs for public schools in Philadelphia. He tells the story of how his mother, who had ambitions to be a lawyer, was told in her first classes in an inner-city public high school that a smart girl like her would make an excellent bank teller. It was an example of the limited horizons presented to many inner-city youths. "So, a bank teller she became. She woke up one day in her forties and said, 'I deserve better. I'm going back to college.' I watched my mother, after years of not being in school, go back to college, powering through the struggle."

Miles was inspired by his mother's chutzpah to rise above the messages she had been fed that kept her down. But what his mother's experience truly ignited in him was the desire to create opportunities for the kids whose ambitions might also be extinguished by being told what they could and couldn't do. "No one's having a conversation with them about what makes them incredible or where the next opportunity might be. All we talk about with black or brown kids is 'a safe place to be.' That is completely unacceptable." Miles wanted to provide enrichment, exposure, and encouragement to those kids. And so, his passion is the purpose that propels EducationWorks to do just that.

CREATING THE RIGHT CULTURE

"The right culture" is a network of values, behaviors, and actions that reinforce the purpose and mission of the organization. Without a clear sense of purpose and mission, the organization's culture lacks strength and cohesiveness, and varies from work unit to work unit.

Vincent talks mission and the importance of culture in the context of relationships with his company's customers and with one another. He said his competitors don't focus on culture. "They focus on the technical, but here, people know how to work together. People have each other's back. That comes from the culture." Vincent is effusive about this being a competitive advantage. He told me, "We have opportunities to lift out talent from the biggest banks in the world. People are looking for an opportunity in an organization where they're relevant, and our basic premise is to make sure every staff member feels like they are important, and they are." Further, Vincent sees the culture as the reason that they are able to fulfill their mission, that is, to be the financial organization that knows how to work with you and that has your back.

"I spend more time than most of my male colleagues do connecting back to purpose and attention to culture. Men that I've worked for, and others, were very focused on objective results."

When I asked the executive men I was interviewing how they differ from other male leaders they've worked with, they said that they care about culture more than other men. Emmet, hospital system CEO, said, "I spend more time than most of my male colleagues do connecting back to purpose and attention to culture. Men that I've worked for, and others, were very focused on objective results."

Paul, our CEO of a nonprofit provider of behavioral and educational services, takes more pride in the influence he has had on the culture of the organization than the financial results.

He said, "I know my leadership has a huge impact on how things happen. So, when I see us hitting our financial metrics, when I see service happening in a really high-quality way, and I see our positive nurturing environment with good staff retention, I feel a personal connection and ownership of them. I get a sense of satisfaction when my colleagues at every level of the organization feel invested in the way that I do."

Paul says, "The business outcome helps me feel good. But it's when others are joining in on that feeling good, that's when I feel great. That is the mark of success and a great culture." The purpose of their business is providing a nurturing environment for an underserved demographic for behavioral health. Paul and his leadership team work to provide that same nurturing environment for their coworkers, being true to their purpose.

Tim, CEO of a statewide community health center system, sees the right culture as the core of his organization's success too, and he has deliberately reinforced it through his collaborative leadership, thinking that works best in the community health center setting. Tim is quite gratified by what he sees as the result of his attention to culture. He proudly told me, "We are in the top one hundred best workplaces in our state, and we've achieved that four times out of the last eight years. That is important to me."

STEWARDING THE CULTURE

The right culture doesn't just sustain itself without the attentive watch of leaders at all levels throughout the organization. Collaborative male leaders embrace their role as steward of the culture, ensuring its integrity and alignment with the purpose and mission of their organization. They ensure that everyone's actions are in line with the culture, knowing that what internal people experience—what is valued inside the organization—is what they will deliver to people externally.

How do collaborative leaders do this?

Emmet believes you have to be "relentless about cultural expectations," that it is a top down and bottom up process. He also recognizes that culture sends a message to employees and customers/patients alike. He said, "By establishing those cultural expectations in a meaningful way, you're meeting the needs of your own team members internally so that they can meet the needs of the people that you're serving."

The executive men in this study talked about the importance of their responsibility to guard the culture they have established. They drive for trust and transparency and remove leaders who act counter to the companies' values.

Neil, our healthcare system CEO, is committed to increasing diversity and sees the organization's culture as an important component of achieving that goal. He doesn't give anyone a pass for not aligning their values with those of the organization. He said, "If some leader, executive, or board member or employee wants to challenge me on why we are committed to eliminating disparities or why we're committed to having a neutral, respectful environment, have at it. I'm going to win that battle all the time. This is not about doing something that's personally good for just me. It's good for our community, the people we serve. It's good for the people that work here. And quite frankly, if you don't value inclusion, you don't value diversity, and you aren't respectful of your colleagues and your patients; you don't belong in this family; there's not a place for you here."

Emmet says he is not only relentless about cultural expectations; he is also vigilant about curtailing naysayers. Even so-called "rainmakers" are not spared. He told me, "We said, 'This is how you're going to show up, or we've got to get you out.' It was all about the behavioral expectations and what was not acceptable."

Both Neil and Emmet emphasized their stance on getting people to align with the organization's values but did not dwell on how they "exited" the people who did not comply. Instead, their focus was on holding people accountable to behavioral expectations and "nudging them" to change, and in some cases, they did. In talking about the danger of turning a blind eye to undesirable behavior, Emmet said, "All it takes is one other senior C-suite executive who doesn't quite buy in, or does not exemplify those

> *"All it takes is one other senior C-suite executive who doesn't quite buy in, or does not exemplify those behaviors or hold their people accountable to those behaviors, and it instantly begins to erode the broader faith and trust and confidence in the overall culture."*

behaviors or hold their people accountable to those behaviors, and it instantly begins to erode the broader faith and trust and confidence in the overall culture. It begins to erode who we say we are, versus who people actually experience we are."

SHAPING THE CULTURE OF THE INDUSTRY AND BEYOND

While collaborative male leaders embrace their role as steward of the culture, no matter their level in the organization, those in the C-suite see their role as not just a steward of their own organization's culture, they also work to improve the ethos of their industry and business community. They speak at industry conferences and events about issues such as diversity and inclusion, mentoring the next generation of leaders, corporate governance, and fostering an ethical culture.

In addition to speaking frequently about the opioid crisis, Neil takes the opportunity to talk to external audiences about diversity in his industry. "I was feeling a little rambunctious, and I looked out at the crowd from the stage, and what I saw was a typical healthcare crowd, mostly white men. I said, 'I have a different view of this audience from up here than everybody else in this room. This looks like a classic healthcare conference, and there's not a community that we serve that looks like this.' I said, 'If we don't do something intentionally to change the makeup in this room in the next five years, we will have failed our community.'"

Neil also pointed out, "Quite frankly, it's pretty easy for a white guy to say these things because no one's going to say I have a chip on my shoulder. It's much easier for me to be a proponent for some of these things as a leader, as a majority leader, than it would be for an African American or LGBTQ individual or some other disenfranchised member of our community, because many of them would be immediately dismissed." Because of this, Neil feels it's his duty to speak out. And when someone in the majority speaks up, it accelerates change.

Collaborative male CEOs have a platform and feel obliged to use it well. It is important to note that they are not doing it just to be in the spotlight, although for some of the men I interviewed, they admitted that it gave them a refreshing ego boost.

Stephen put it out there to me this way, "I feed my ego by presenting around the world. I just came back from Brazil and am going to Turkey, then Australia. I am the go-to guy in the US." He truly is considered the global expert in his field and is committed to educating people on what he and his organization have learned. He feels that he is helping shape the future of the industry and is very proud that he can hold his own with PhDs and MDs in the audience, even though, much to his chagrin, he doesn't hold those advanced degrees. He made me laugh talking about preparing for these big conferences. He said, "I do the same presentation over and over, but the night before, like at one in the morning, I'll think of a funny story to add or something I want to change up a little. So, I'm up and working on the slides in the middle of the night." He grins mischievously and says, "I do it every time."

All leaders pay attention to having an "executive presence" that is consistent with their role; collaborative male CEOs took that further. They talked about their ever awareness that they are the face of their organization, that they are an embodiment, if you will, of what the organization is about. Just as they are ever mindful of tending the culture in their organization, they are mindful of presenting themselves in a way that is consistent with that culture. As Emmet, our healthcare CEO who had the off-site for thirteen thousand employees, said, "You're onstage all the time, whether you're in the work environment or you're in the community, you are the standard by which the organization is going to be judged by people within the organization or outside of it. They look to you to see what's acceptable and what's not acceptable."

□□□

Collaborative male leaders drive their organizations to success by continually reinforcing its purpose and mission and by nurturing the culture. With commitment and passion, they engage those inside and outside the organization. Their collaborative approach and focus on the purpose of their business gives people in their charge a greater sense of self-efficacy and trust, allowing the organization to be nimbler in dealing with changes in their business environment. In their attention to purpose, these leaders create a sense of "we" and promote meaningfulness where people feel they are contributing to a greater cause.

More than other leaders, they place higher importance on the culture than other metrics. They think that if they keep the culture healthy and strong, the bottom-line results will follow. As such, they are stewards of the culture within, and they are proponents of improving the culture of their industry.

CHAPTER 8

Clinch Commitment: Cultivating Shared Accountability

"A genuine leader is not a searcher for consensus but a molder of consensus."

—Martin Luther King Jr.

Driving accountability in the organization is imperative to achieving company goals. This can present a challenge for collaborative leaders in that "holding people accountable" has traditionally been seen as a directive action by someone of higher rank. Collaborative male leaders reinforce accountability, but they do it differently than their hierarchical "carrot and stick"-using counterparts. They center on purpose and build common support for the goals, assisting people who are struggling, and use the whole team to feel and accept responsibility for each other. They practice servant leadership, taking responsibility to support others and to help them reach their goals.

Our publisher CEO, Andrew, said his boss, a member of the executive committee on the board, was a believer in "holding their feet to the fire," but he wasn't going to do it that way. It's not his style. He said, "For me, management is like

"For me, management is like being a good coach. I told my boss, 'Let me tell you the difference. When they're in trouble, I get up from this side of the table, and I go sit next to them. I say, "How can I help you?"'"

being a good coach. I told my boss, 'Let me tell you the difference. When they're in trouble, I get up from this side of the table, and I go sit next to them. I say, "How can I help you?"'" Andrew works with people who aren't "meeting their numbers" in order to figure out with them how they can be successful, and he regularly follows up to ensure positive progress.

Tim, our CEO of a community healthcare system, expressed his concern about "having an edge," meaning that he was reluctant to pressure people who did not meet a goal. He told me, "People on the board thought I'm too nice, too lenient, or it's too easy just to walk over Tim." So, he was coached to ensure people knew that there were serious consequences for not meeting an objective. His fear, however, was that it would not be consistent with who he said he aspires to be, that is, a servant leader. He came to realize, though, that maintaining accountability is a critical component of servant leadership when it is a two-way street, and that shared approach was effective and fit very well with who he is as a person and who he is as a leader.

ACHIEVING SERVANT LEADERSHIP

Servant leadership was first introduced in the 1970s by Robert Greenleaf, a retired AT&T director of management, who found that the power-centered authoritarian leadership style prominent in America's large institutions was not working. He discovered that the organizations that had sustainable success had leaders who acted more as supportive coaches and served both the needs of employees and the organization. He founded the Greenleaf Center for Servant Leadership.

As you would guess, servant leadership is about thinking "service first," making sure the highest priority needs of people you lead are being served. The Marine Corps adopted this model, calling it service-based leadership, and it is at the center of their culture. When you unpack how servant leaders are described, it sounds remarkably like the leadership characteristics identified in this book. They collaborate, mentor, and give of themselves for the betterment of others. They are regarded as humble.

Dan Cable, professor of organizational behavior at London Business School and author of *Alive at Work*,[19] says that humility and servant leadership don't imply an attitude of servility. Instead, Cable emphasizes that it's the leader's "responsibility to increase ownership, autonomy, and responsibility of followers— to encourage them to think for themselves and try out their own ideas." Increasing the responsibility of others includes holding them accountable to meet those responsibilities.

The concept of leaders pivoting between directing and supporting in order to increase ownership and responsibility can be demonstrated using David Kantor's Four Player Model.[20] A team leader can assume four different conversational stances to move their group to take action. Leaders shift from a "mover" stance to set the stage and initiate goal-setting discussions, to a "bystander" stance to allow and observe participation, to an "opposer" stance to ask critical questions (perhaps "play the devil's advocate"), to a "follower" stance as the group moves closer toward consensus. This model for leadership assumes a balance of accountability among the team members and their leader.

HANDLING PUSHBACK FROM AUTHORITARIAN MALE LEADERS

Both Tim and Andrew, CEOs running different operations, have had to deal with men in higher level roles pressuring them to be more demanding. Nick, our empathetic general counsel, has also been told by male peers that he is "too kind."

Craig, senior VP of an information technology giant, also feels pressured. He told me, "I think men respect other men. They make fun of you if you're a little too compassionate. When you get your hackles up and say, 'Back off, this is why I'm doing what I'm doing,' and you tie it to business, they let up. It's not about being lovey-dovey or because it's the right thing to do. It's because I respect my people, and it's good for the business." He went on to say that he thought testosterone was driving the behavior of guys who act like that, and he counters it with intellect rather than machismo. Although, I couldn't help but notice that he also "got his hackles up" to aggressively punctuate his intellectual counterpunch.

"I think men respect other men. They make fun of you if you're a little too compassionate. When you get your hackles up and say, 'Back off, this is why I'm doing what I'm doing,' and you tie it to business, they let up."

Given that there is a global pressure for men to be "tough" and "self-reliant," it isn't surprising that men in leadership who coach rather than give ultimatums, who depend on others rather than be decisively independent, who are compassionate not callous, get pushback to toughen up. However, at the C-suite level, these collaborative male leaders apparently have the cred and the confidence to "do it their way."

Cultivating shared accountability for collaborative leaders means that they uphold their end of the bargain by providing what others need to meet their objectives. For every goal and initiative under their watch, collaborative leaders work with those responsible to identify reciprocal goals. They do it by collaboratively setting goals. The leader has accountabilities, as do those in his charge. As Andrew says, he asks, "How can I help you?"

Craig also takes the "how-can-I-help-you" stance. He expects the best of others, so he sees their shortcomings as a problem to fix together with them. He said, "Some of my colleagues feel that people left to their own devices are inherently lazy and incapable of doing anything unless you micromanage them." But Craig assumes just the opposite. He said, "There are very few people who are just inherently lazy, who don't want to do a good job. Everybody wants to do a good job. Everybody wants to be recognized for what they do. So, figuring out a way to make sure that they're able to express their talents and their passions is my job as a leader."

LEVERAGING SHARED ACCOUNTABILITY IN BUSINESS TURNAROUNDS

Patrick found that cultivating shared accountability was critical to business turnarounds, since at the root of fixing the business was fixing the team. He said, "I made sure that there was clarity around each and everybody's roles contributing to the greater win. And then we had a cadence that we would build, and I'd start to realize that like any sports team that I was a part of, we would literally rebuild the team with an aggressive look at turning the business around."

When Patrick went into these turnaround situations, he focused on getting the group into a "cadence" where inter-dependencies around goals were established. He said, "I'd see people working against each other and you know, the first thing I did was try to fix it. It was siloed, very individualistic; you know, everybody was out for themselves. There was a lot of backstabbing going on. There wasn't a strategy and no disci-plined cadence around how to get things done."

> *He focused on getting the group into a "cadence" where interdependencies around goals were established.*

Patrick also focused on each individual and rather point-edly emphasized their need to take responsibility for change. He said, "As I was picking people from my team, and they would explain to me why they wanted to be part of the team, I was like, 'Man, are you sure? Because it's going to be hard, since in order for me to help you reach this aspiration, you're going to need to develop. Let's agree that there are some things that are going to need to change.'" But with that message, he fueled others' efforts by expressing confidence in them that they *could* do it. He told me, "The balance point was always getting people to believe that I really expect that they can do it, knowing that they would go home and complain to their significant other, 'That dude's crazy.'"

Leaders cultivate accountability by making it a reciprocal imperative, by sharing goals and insisting that they themselves be held accountable by their people. Patrick developed the strategy with the team, and they collaboratively set goals and individual accountabilities, including what *his* accountabilities were. It's a teamwork skill defining "what's mine, yours, ours." Not only did it encourage buy-in to a shared mission, but the collaborative goal setting ensured that people were not working at cross purposes and competing among themselves. He continued, "I said to them, 'Are you prepared to do this? Because I'm going to hold you accountable, and I'm holding me accountable. Show you have accountability around how we're going to get this stuff done and tell me what you need from me.' So there was, you know, this idea that what I worked for was for them."

Patrick didn't use the term "servant leadership," but it certainly sounded a lot like it. He made his level of commitment to his teams clear, saying, "Are you willing to give of yourself, not just in time, but around trust and development? We're gonna invest in each other."

Dane, our senior VP in technology and communications and former Marine, is another leader who faced a couple of business turnarounds. He approached those situations figuring out what he could do to enable his team. He said, "I would say my core philosophy is one of servant leadership. When you give people space but don't give them the tools they need, the resources they need, but say they have to deliver, that's poor leadership. That definitely comes from my marine training."

He told me about a particular situation that was "a mess." He said, "I discovered they weren't organized at all. And for me, that comes back to leadership. I thought, who's holding them accountable for delivering these things and enabling them to deliver? Who's giving them what they need, but also holding them accountable to that?"

Dane replaced the leader of the team with a new vice president, Beth, who also believed in reciprocal accountability. He said "From that point on, everything was on time and on budget. But two interesting things happened early on. When the first milestone was due, Beth came back to me and said, 'We're not going to make it.' I said, 'Yes, you are. What do you need to figure out a way? There's a way.'"

Dane and Beth worked together to figure out a way, and they did make the deadline. But a month later, the team said they were going to miss the second milestone. He said, "I was like, no, no, no. Then it dawned on me that they were asking permission to fail, and I wouldn't do that. I think it was about the group culture where it was okay to miss deadlines, and there were no consequences. Nobody ever got fired. They just pushed it out and would try again. There was no accountability."

Dane made the distinction about being a servant leader and indiscriminately providing resources. He said, "I've seen so many leaders just throw money at things. But without holding people accountable for results, you get into those ongoing spirals. Beth, however, swapped some people out to get the 'right team' together and did hold them accountable. They did what they needed to do and exceeded their goal."

Craig also had an imperative to rescue a business that was in trouble. Before accepting the leadership role, he investigated what was going on. "I found out that the Commonwealth of Kentucky was close to suing us for breach of contract. So was Wyoming. We were severely behind in product development. We signed contracts where the salespeople sold things that weren't near completion. The only way I was able to describe the seriousness of the situation to other people in our company was that there were mushroom clouds going off all over the country." Having told them what he found, Craig said, "They were like, 'Here you go, Craig; have at it; have a good day.' Wow. So, the first thing in my mind, and it was more instinctual than anything else, was, 'You better have a great leadership team and the team of people ought to be really good.'"

Working together with his leadership team, they unpacked the problem. "The first thing we did was head to the war room and brainstorm. How long is it really going to take to finish these builds we are doing? From what we were contractually committed, it wasn't even close. There's no way. It was already a year behind schedule. No matter how good of a negotiator I was, I wasn't able to go to a client and say, 'Do you mind waiting for another year?' So, we said, 'Okay, how are we going to do this in a short period of time? We're going to have to buy or align with someone.' The three of us really hammered it out. We still had to build a user interface and some integration. And, in order for the solution to be competitive, in order for it to meet most of the requirements that we committed to in our contracts, we had to work with companies where we had good relationships."

Rather than try to outline a solution himself, Craig believed that he needed his team to participate fully in evaluating the situation, making decisions together, putting a project plan in place to get there and agreeing on milestones. But he didn't stop there in how he shared accountability; he was all in. "These people walked through fire because I did it with them, stayed up late with them. I made sure they had the right people around them too, the right resources to get done what they needed to get done."

Craig secured reliable assistance by bringing in outside colleagues who would share accountability with him and his internal team. "I had some very trusted partners that I worked with at my previous company. And so I didn't have to perform technical or business due diligence. It allowed me to very quickly establish partnerships, negotiate business relationships and discounts and other things. It allowed us to bring to market a hybrid product that was part of what our partners put together and part of what we did."

In the end, Craig's team did turn it around thanks to his ability to convene others and create shared accountability, not just within his group, but also with outside relationships. He talked about Kentucky in particular. "We made it not too much past the date that the amended contract stated. The functionality was actually enhanced. We went from being thrown out to being embraced." He grinned and told me that in appreciation, the governor invited them to the Kentucky Derby.

BUILDING A RELATIONSHIP NETWORK

Cultivating shared accountability depends on building relationships in order to understand the needs of the people in your charge, as was evident with Patrick. But taking it to a higher level, proactively developing a network of relationships allows leaders to take a collegial approach to maintaining accountability. Collaborative leaders maintain a dialog with their colleagues above, below, and at their peer level, regularly reaching out and keeping up with them.

Dane deliberately builds and maintains a network of relationships. Being that he was an IT guy, I found it particularly amusing that he developed a spreadsheet to systematically ensure that he connects with everyone in his network regularly.

Of course he would, right? "I have a spreadsheet with a list of names and of the frequency I need to touch base with them. I'll put it on my calendar, for thirty minutes or whatever, just to touch base and see how the kids are doing and make those connections. And it's worked wonders for me."

He was proud of the fact that he had a reputation for being great at maintaining relationships and has helped others reporting to him by "giving them the spreadsheet lecture" so they had an easy tool to build and maintain their networks. Dane thinks that creating a lattice of relationships enables him to hold people accountable in a collegial way. It's really more about *maintaining* accountability.

Dane thinks that creating a lattice of relationships enables him to hold people accountable in a collegial way. It's really more about maintaining accountability.

The self-developed system Dane created reminded me of Vincent, who makes a list every Monday of people he hasn't seen in a while. For him, it was about maintaining a collaborative, supportive culture. But a necessary part of that culture is shared accountability; they are accountable to one another; they "have each other's back." Vincent said, "One-on-one lunches keep me on my toes. I ask, 'What should I be doing for you? What am I missing?'" He maintained accountability by systematically staying in touch and soliciting suggestions on how he could better serve them as a leader.

Using a relationship network reminded me of the "coconut wireless" that Ikaika and his team expanded and relied on to collaboratively maintain accountability for all aspects of their relief efforts during the volcanic eruption.

BUILDING DECISION CAPITAL

Rafael, our empathetic CEO of a biological services organization, saw building and maintaining a network as a critical safety net during times when the business is not looking rosy. He talked about a quality control crisis that got the organization in trouble with industry regulators. "One of our departments was operating so terribly. The board appreciated the way that we reacted to it versus what exactly happened. And so, they're behind us a hundred and fifty percent, and we're working through these things. I think the only way you do that is by having built decision capital."

Decision capital, as Rafael described it, is the result of a long-term, comprehensive effort to surround yourself with people who are aligned with you, who you constantly include to have input in any decisions that need to be made. In the case of the quality control issue facing Rafael's organization, he was open with his board, laid out the issues, and solicited their input as he plotted a course of action. He kept them aware of the actions that they were taking. When things didn't work out as anticipated, the board didn't blame Rafael.

"When you've invested in those partnerships and relation-ships, you get the benefit of the doubt when something like this happens. If you're reclusive, and you have a big ego, and you only involve people when it's convenient for you or when you're feeling too much pressure about a particular decision, then people are less willing to rally around you or behind you to help you get through it and come to the solution. There've been CEOs that have been confronted with tough issues like this, but if they alienated everybody around them, when this happens, it only becomes an opportunity for them to get rid of you."

So, building decision capital involves being inclusive, particularly in decision making, and especially over time. Demonstrating that you are thinking about the right things, time and time again, you get the benefit of the doubt when things go wrong, as they will.

□□□

Collaborative male leaders are servant leaders who provide what others need to meet their objectives. They are engaged with their teams, shoulder-to-shoulder, to achieve what sometimes feels impossible. They are able to "hold people accountable" by leveraging the relationships they have with them.

Collaborative leaders build a network of relationships to keep up and stay connected with others, even if they are not currently working toward a shared goal. For example, establishing a lattice of relationships was the secret to success for Ikaika during the eruption. His network, "the coconut wireless," had built capital for the future, so he was able to reach out easily when he needed it. And like Craig, who saved a disastrous situation, said about his network, "they walked through fire" for him. Well, in Ikaika's case, they walked through lava. What cultivating shared accountability boils down to is relationships and inclusiveness; they are the glue that builds it and holds it together.

CHAPTER 9

Tend to Talent: Developing Future Leaders

"Leaders don't create more followers, they create more leaders."

–Tom Peters

Perhaps because of their inclusive style, collaborative male leaders actively mentor and coach their direct reports and others in the organization. They involve them in problem solving and decision making; they share their thought processes with them (which, after all, is what mentoring and coaching is all about). As a result, in addition to the positive impact collaborative leadership has on the culture and productivity of the organization, a natural outcome of that style is the professional development of future leaders and of individual contributors. In the case of many male leaders, this is dependent on them tempering their ego. Of course it is! Successful coaching and mentoring necessitate an outward focus; they require listening, empathy, respect, and other relationship-building skills, whereas ego is about cultivating "me." Some leaders conflate the two.

We know when we are dealing with someone with a big ego. They aren't tuned into us. They aren't asking us about our thoughts and experiences. Even when we insert our perspectives, they aren't listening to them. We aren't truly having a dialogue, but rather, we're getting their monologue. They are on their own stage, standing in the spotlight, often reminding us that they are in the spotlight and how wonderful that is. We find ourselves feeling uncomfortably obligated to show that we are impressed by them. It's aggravating and pathetic all at the same time.

Their way of developing people is to tell them "how it's done," elaborating with varying degrees of grandiosity about what they did to get to their position. They probably believe that this is an effective way of coaching and developing others. But it's like teaching someone how to drive by letting them watch you drive from the back seat. You will have no feel for how much pressure is required on the gas pedal to accelerate smoothly or on the brake to stop without a jolt. You won't have the chance to try an action and get feedback indicating the impact of that action.

A collaborative leader gives you the wheel, sitting next to you to offer guidance. And although they may offer stories to illustrate lessons they learned while driving, they keep the focus on the student, their questions, their skills, and areas for improvement. They keep their ego in check and let others shine. We saw this demonstrated in the chapter Tempering Ego.

The executives I interviewed were avid developers of talent. They not only saw it as a responsibility of their role, they got deep personal satisfaction from helping people grow. Their focus on growing leadership talent was in fact their number one priority and was consistently cited as their top professional accomplishment.

When I asked Dane to talk about a high point for him in the last two years, he spoke with pride about having cultivated effective leaders, thereby bolstering his department. About one of his direct reports, Beth, who he had developed for a leadership role, he said, "For years, nobody else could do what she did, and many tried. She put the right structure and process in place, put the right people in place, developed people." He went on to say, "Multiple directors were promoted to vice president under my watch. And some were previously considered to be problem children, damaged goods. But I got there, worked with them, and turned all that around."

GIVING THEM SPACE TO FAIL

Charles, who gave his executive assistant the opportunity to present to the board, believes in "giving the wheel" to people so they learn. He told me about his COO, who he is deliberately developing for his job. "I will actually watch her fail, in an instructive, not a mean-spirited way. The only way she's going to learn is if I allow space for her to make her own decisions. She'll say, 'What do you think I should do?' and I'll say back to her, 'You're the Chief Operating Officer, it's your decision.' I can't always be saying, 'Hey, I did this in '06. I've seen this before. This is exactly what you have to do.' If she fails, I say, 'Alright, let's move on. What did we learn from that? How do you pivot?' It's a very hard thing as a leader to not intervene. It is difficult to just let go. When it is high stakes for the company, I don't."

Similarly, Nick talked about stepping back to let one of his direct reports learn. "I have to park my ego. I have to bite my tongue sometimes when I know what they're doing is not quite the right way to go. I have to let them figure a lot out for themselves because that's how I learned."

Of course, Charles' decision to step in, or Nick's decision to stand back, is based on a risk analysis of consequences that he is willing or not willing to accept. They don't swoop in and take over when a problem occurs; they let people learn from their mistakes and learn how to work themselves out of a difficult problem.

"I have to park my ego. I have to bite my tongue sometimes when I know what they're doing is not quite the right way to go. I have to let them figure a lot out for themselves because that's how I learned."

TUNING INTO TALENT INDICATORS

Collaborative male leaders appear to have an eye for seeing potential in others. This could very well be a function of empathy and listening. Often, it is a matter of paying attention to relevant behavioral competencies that may have been developed through a variety of life experiences and recognizing these as transferable skills. It is also the result of watching people to whom they have delegated in action. This ability to tune into talent helps leaders make good choices for filling important leadership roles, a vital part of the succession planning and management process.

Remember our story of Dane and Beth who got a troubled team to deliver on time and on budget? Beth had the skill to build the right team, support its members, and hold them accountable, even though she lacked the technical background. He said, "I pulled her in from another part of the company to replace the team leader who was not organized and was not enabling the team to deliver. I recommended that she be promoted to VP. She was an Olympic coach for the Australian swimming team and has run the Boston marathon a number of times. I thought, 'Perfect.' She got in there a little bit over her head at first; it was a complex situation for her to sort through, but that's okay. She kept going and was an active coach to them, and she delivered." Dane had seen that Beth had the drive and the goal orientation to lead the team to be effective.

When Vincent was conducting a search to fill a new leadership role in his company, he put his support behind a particular candidate, Jeremy—a decision that did not seem as clear-cut to others. He explained the leadership challenge the candidate would face, saying, "As is common with bank-owned insurance companies, it's a bunch of acquisitions that we've made to get a business from as far south as Virginia to New York State. It's almost like we are running eighteen different little insurance agencies. I need a leader who can take eighteen different sales processes and cultures and roll them into one. He needs to create discipline and marketing consistency in order to create a single franchise within this footprint and expand." Vincent saw that Jeremy was an orchestrator and connector, qualities he had clearly demonstrated in his current job.

Vincent told me that he got some pushback from his CEO, who thought that it might be too big of a jump for Jeremy to step into this leadership role. Although Jeremy was from a much larger organization and had successfully integrated five business entities there, the integration was not of the scale Vincent needed. But Vincent made a strong argument for why they should take the chance with Jeremy, explaining the competencies this candidate brought to the table. "He's been through this dynamic of needing to integrate different acquisitions, so he's got a track record of building a team from disparate work groups. And he also has sales leadership in his background, and that's where you can make it or break it in this business. We have too big a difference between our poor producers and our good producers, and he's got to get his arms around that and figure out what decisions we need to make."

TAPPING INTO BROADER DATA

Despite the wisdom of best practices about using competency criteria for selection of job candidates, executives I interviewed said there was something else that came into play when considering the right person for a job. Vincent told me, "I hate to say it, but it's a gut feeling. It really is. You can read books that say to never go with gut feelings, but I have been fortunate to have made some extremely strong hires that way. I believe in conversations where you immediately can tell if someone is right for your organization or not. Not that I don't make a mistake from time to time, but most of the time I get it right."

I would argue that what Vincent described as "gut feelings" *are* based on data. However, there are some people who describe a gut feeling or instinct that goes against existing data; in that case, they are just showing self-assured hubris. Collaborative leaders are listeners, and they are empathetic, which allows them to get a good a sense of who a person is, what they care about, and how they interact. They also respect others, which means they are open to considering people who may not have the perfect

With these characteristics, leaders have access to more data than their non-collaborative colleagues. They can see what others don't because they tune into information that is subtle.

resume. So, with these characteristics, leaders have access to more data than their non-collaborative colleagues. They can see what others don't because they tune into information that is subtle.

GETTING OTHERS' PERSPECTIVES

Despite their more comprehensive view of a candidate, collaborative leaders don't go it alone. After all, that would be antithetical to their nature. Also, it would be politically unwise to not get buy-in from other stakeholders in the organization—not just to cover one's butt as it were, but to ensure that the candidate has the best possible chance to succeed there. Vincent said, "I also have other people weigh in, leaders who look at it from different angles and who will think differently. I think that diverse views of a candidate are critical." The CEO reconsidered his initial concern that Jeremy wasn't ready, based on Vincent's rationale about Jeremy's skill set. The other leaders Vincent brought in to vet Jeremy also gave him a thumbs-up. Jeremy proved to be an excellent hire, a good fit for the job and for the organization, and an adept unifier of different factions throughout the business.

Collaborative leaders seem to define a successful leader more broadly and consider other behaviors either equally or more important than technical skills or experience in areas directly related to the work. They consider that certain experiences are transferable and, thus, would substitute for direct skills in that industry or functional area. They might also consider that to prepare a person for a higher-level role, they need a different experience that rounds out their portfolio. So even though they don't seem to have all the prerequisites for that new role, they are put in the role to learn and to succeed at the next higher level.

Seeing evidence of transferable skills, paying attention to broader data based on listening and empathy, and soliciting others' perceptions are critical competencies for hiring; those same characteristics also apply to choosing who to coach, develop, and promote within the organization.

LEARNING GOALS, STRENGTHS, AND DEVELOPMENT NEEDS

Effective coaching and mentoring require a leader to proactively solicit others' thoughts about their personal goals. Rather than wait to be sought out, collaborative leaders open the door to conversations about career and professional development. They gauge the level of commitment a person has to their goals, encouraging them but not pushing them beyond what they want to or are willing to do. They help others strategize their path, listening and asking the right questions. They reinforce that professional and personal development is the responsibility of the individual; the leader is there for support.

The collaborative male leaders I interviewed were naturally tuned into others' development since they were focused on their own. Neil told me that he has a passion for lifelong learning. He said, "As a leader you can get yourself into a situation, particularly as a CEO, where you think you've reached the pinnacle. You don't need to learn anymore. And I think that one of the greatest challenges that leaders face is evolving your thinking." Rafael told me that he was interested in participating in my research because it gave him an opportunity to reflect on his development path and what he has learned in the last ten years.

With their focus on professional development, their own and that of others in their organization, it isn't surprising that these collaborative leaders place high importance on succession planning and management. Although boards of publicly traded companies often insist that there is a succession plan for the CEO, as in who would step into that role should the executive "get hit by a bus," it is surprising how many executives don't formally have a talent review, considering not only who could replace them, but how to get that person ready to replace them. Collaborative leaders do.

I have worked with these leaders and their teams to identify individuals who have the potential to advance, what positions they could move into, and how long they need to acquire the knowledge and experience required. But the critical management of succession is to identify the development actions necessary for those individuals who are on succession slates.

The difference between these collaborative male leaders and others who are not collaborative but do succession planning might be a matter of mindset. Carol S. Dweck, Stanford professor of psychology, describes a growth mindset as the belief that abilities can be developed and that the desire to embrace learning, challenges, and setbacks are sources of growth.[21] People with a fixed mindset believe you either are or are not good at something based on your inherent nature. From what I heard from the collaborative leaders in this study, they have a growth mindset, and it fuels their passion for developing others.

In Rafael's organization, for development purposes, he expanded the senior leadership team to include two individuals who did not report directly to him but to one of his direct reports. This gave the individuals access to participate in discussions, debates, and decision making at that top level, building their critical thinking, confidence, and influence.

Stephen, whose organization coordinates organ transplants, ensured that his potential successors—the head of clinical operations and the top administrative officer—got visibility and cultivated credibility with key external stakeholders several years before he intended to step down as CEO. Although Stephen is the "face" of the organization, he considers himself and his two direct reports as a leadership triad. The COO and CAO are fully aligned with him to plan strategy and craft a vision for the future of the organization.

DEVELOPING WOMEN

The executive men I interviewed are particularly committed to developing women for leadership. This is an important theme to explore, given the difficult gender dynamics that have persistently been an issue and that were brought to the forefront by the #MeToo movement, and men's distress in how to work with and develop women for professional advancement.

The commitment of the men in this study to supporting women wasn't a huge surprise, given that they were recommended to me by executive women who worked with them and identified them as successful collaborative leaders. They were described as being someone they admired, someone who supported them and with whom they felt comfortable.

So why might these leaders be committed to developing women?

It may be that they "get it" and see the biases that strong women face. It may also be that they recognize their own collaborative leadership characteristics are the skills that enable women to lead successfully, and, therefore, these men are good role models. Perhaps they, more than other male leaders, recognize women's traits as strengths rather than weaknesses because they share those strengths. It may also be that they developed a deep admiration for strong women earlier in their life and career, something we will discuss later in this book.

I must concede that I may well have heard about these men's efforts to mentor and advocate for women because they "did their homework" on who was interviewing them. If I'd not been a leader in the field of women's leadership, much less a man, perhaps I wouldn't have heard these stories from them. Be that as it may, their mentoring experiences were not fabricated. And, they were proud of their efforts to develop women.

Charles is an advocate for talented women throughout his organization. He said, "We have a manager within our organization who is strong, confident, and does a great job leading her team. But some people who don't buy her are filing complaints with HR. HR came to me and I said, 'Well tell me what she's done wrong.' Turns out, she didn't do anything wrong. Apparently, some people—both men and women—had an issue with a very strong woman who is very clear about what she wants from you, and she's not smiling."

Dane was asked to intervene when a female manager was supposedly overworking people. He stood by her, helping her tweak her behavior and change the perception of the people who worked for her. "She wanted to do it all, and she wanted every *t* crossed, every head bowed. I taught her to discern what is important and make sure that gets done. I said to her, 'Some of the things you think are important today, next week, nobody's going to care about. So be careful that you're not running around spending activity on things that are really hard and may not be that important.' The issue was resolved. She got to the point where she was developing people, and people started going to her, seeking her out as someone they wanted to work for. It was nice to watch."

Letting people learn by doing instead of showing them or doing it for them is a way in which collaborative male leaders can be excellent mentors to women who aren't often offered the opportunity to take the wheel and do a test drive. Nick and Charles are both developing women for the C-suite by letting them make mistakes and learn, as discussed earlier. It is a tricky business, though, because in many leadership roles, women are judged more harshly when they make mistakes.

> *Letting people learn by doing instead of showing them or doing it for them is a way in which collaborative male leaders can be excellent mentors to women who aren't often offered the opportunity to take the wheel and do a test drive.*

Victoria Brescoll, professor at Yale School of Management, showed that women who are employed in jobs that are strongly associated with men—and vice versa—are more severely penalized for making mistakes than those who are in positions associated with their own gender.[22] For example, male women's college presidents and female police chiefs were judged more harshly when they made an error. Brescoll's team concluded that people find it easier to accept a bad decision when it's made by a leader in a "gender-appropriate role."

Alice Eagly, professor of psychology and of management and organizations at Northwestern University, first described "role congruity theory"[23] in her pivotal research conducted nearly twenty years ago where she found that women fared less well in relation to roles with particularly masculine definitions, including executive roles. Eagly says that women face this disadvantage of not being seen as effective because of a disconnect that people perceive between the description of gender and leader roles. She says, "This blending produces the perception that women, compared with equivalent men, possess less agency [ambitious, courageous] and more communion [affectionate, emotional] and therefore are less qualified for leadership, especially for executive roles." Eagly and other researchers have consistently found this to be the case, even recently, despite gender stereotypes shifting over time.[24]

Herminia Ibarra, professor of organizational behavior at London Business School, has found that women are still perceived as "risky" appointments for executive roles by often male-dominated committees.[25] The biases that we see in Brescoll's study suggest that putting a man in these high-level jobs is seen as less of a risk because a mistake will be forgiven more readily than it would be for a woman. Studies have also shown that when women fail in a role dominated by men, it reinforces the expectation that she isn't suited for the role. That bias can be a deterrent for promoting women. This means that mentoring women for the C-suite must include sponsoring them and being an advocate for them at the highest levels.

Mentoring women for the C-suite must include sponsoring them and being an advocate for them at the highest levels.

Despite these issues, the collaborative men I interviewed seemed to be open to developing everyone who works for them, not only people who fit the profile of current leaders in their organization.

APPLYING POLITICAL AND EMOTIONAL SAVVY IN DEVELOPMENT

When Dane sponsored Beth, the person who turned around a non-productive team, he focused on increasing her visibility with his peers across the company and helping her build connections. When I asked how he facilitated that, he said, "There were specific people that I asked her to 'put on her list' to reach out to. Behind the scenes I talked with the more senior people and said, 'Hey, I'm sending this person to you. She really could use a mentor.' There were a couple of senior women in particular I talked with saying, 'I can't give her the perspective you can give her. I need you to do that. I can give her a white male over fifty perspective, but I can guarantee you that my experience has been different than yours is as a senior vice president, a woman coming through finance. She needs mentors like that in addition to me.'"

Interestingly, Dane focused specifically on connecting Beth with Sarah, a woman who was running all of the call centers. Although Sarah was well regarded by most of the company, Beth didn't particularly like her. "She just didn't know her, so they would pass each other in the hallway without a word, and they just never broke through that initial distance. So, when I found out that Sarah was going to a two-week development course at Harvard, I maneuvered to have them go together, and they came back best buddies." Dane said that Sarah became a good mentor. "You can't leave this stuff to chance. To balance relationships that will help you deliver what you want is critical. And Beth was having some confidence issues, so making that connection helped. I just encouraged her and supported her publicly."

It would be negligent not to address the difficulty that has always existed and that has become heightened in the recent years of #MeToo with senior-level men sponsoring and developing more junior women. The gender dynamics in the workplace, for all levels of an organization, have changed drastically over the last thirty years, even over the last ten. A September 2018 Harris Poll survey of 472 men working full-time concluded that 75 percent of men are paralyzed with fear about how to work with women. Some male leaders have confided in me that it is just too difficult to navigate coaching, mentoring, and sponsoring women. One man said, "I just can't risk it." The Harris Poll confirmed that men are pulling back from interacting with women, just to "play it safe."

Collaborative male leaders are great mentors to emerging female leaders because they are emotionally savvy.

Collaborative male leaders are great mentors to emerging female leaders because they are emotionally savvy; their feelings serve them well in being able to feel and demonstrate empathy. They have also mastered managing their emotions and not crossing a line.

How are they able to do this? They have a strong moral compass, understanding that the power differential between themselves and a more junior-level woman makes a more intimate relationship taboo. Though this doesn't mean that they don't connect emotionally; they do. But they are also attuned to how people react to them.

They are aware that some women may have their guard up, and so they are sensitive to making those women feel more at ease by maintaining a situation-appropriate emotional distance.

Their ability to do this and build trust is a direct result of empathy. Another shared characteristic that serves collaborative male leaders well as they mentor women is that they have a tremendous regard for them. As I noted earlier and discuss in the next chapter, they often developed a deep admiration for strong women from a young age. They relate to them and their difficulties as being a woman leader. As one executive man told me, it's about respect.

BRINGING UP THE MIDDLE

Sponsorship and development aren't just for executive candidates; the men I interviewed cast a broader net in their endeavors to grow future leaders. Talent review cascades down through the top few levels of the organization. Collaborative leaders aren't focused on an organizational process such as succession planning but, instead, are more focused on developing people in their organization. They tend to engage a broader group of people in their day-to-day operations. They get to know the individuals' strengths and development needs and can provide them with opportunities to grow.

Andrew, our publishing CEO, focuses on supporting professional development of millennials. For example, he regularly emphasizes to them the importance of the company's mission to uphold freedom of speech and to promote diversity. He wants to ensure that everyone growing with the company is on board to hear all voices—women, men, liberal, conservative, racial and ethnic minorities.

We have seen multiple examples throughout this book of these collaborative male leaders connecting with people, even below the level that would be included in talent review for succession planning. Some seem driven by empathy, such as Nick, who sponsored learning opportunities for legal assistants so they could advance and earn more. For him and others, seeing people succeed boosted their egos and made them feel good about their ability to make a difference in someone's career.

When I asked Dane how he thought his leadership style differs from other men he has worked with, he talked about the amount of time he spends developing people for leadership. He said, "I'm pulling them in one-on-one, asking 'What's working? What's not working? How do we make a better you?'" But in addition to taking more time with people, Dane also made it a point to not view development as a process to "fix" a potential leader. He said, "I use an analogy around thinking about development. Say you were a jar; your jar is full of stuff. I don't want to change what's in the jar. I try to give you new perspectives or new capabilities and insights that make you more effective and help you grow. Development is a journey, a constant process, not a destination."

□⊓⊔

Collaborative male leaders are superb creators of future leaders. They take great pride and get delight from developing others. They have a keen eye for emerging talent. With their empathy and listening, they pick up on characteristics and strengths in others that may be missed by their peers. Collaborative male leaders have the know-how and commitment to developing women for leadership. They give people a chance to "take the wheel" and analyze failures and successes. These men are devoted to lifelong learning and continued development for themselves and those in their charge.

PART THREE

DEVELOPING AND LEADING WITH THE MEN'S NEW LEADERSHIP BLUEPRINT

CHAPTER 10

The Making of a Collaborative Male Leader

"I am not a product of my circumstances. I am a product of my decisions."

–Stephen R. Covey

Now that we have described the benefits and explored the key traits of collaborative male leadership, the big question is how do men develop those traits? How do they get to be empathetic, humble, respecting of all, at ease with vulnerability, and nurturers and cultivators of shared accountability? How have men developed these values and behaviors?

Many collaborative male leaders come by their leadership style organically. They had experiences in their early life that set in motion this particular way of navigating the world. A large proportion in this category cited the heavy influence of women in their childhood: single mothers, grandmothers, or sisters.

Other leaders I interviewed developed their style by watching those around them, trying on behaviors that they admired and fit their personality or rejecting behaviors they did not see as worthy examples of effectiveness.

What all of these collaborative leaders had in common was that they observed, listened, and learned from others as they progressed in their lives. They were open to bringing these lessons into themselves and continuing to grow as a person and a leader.

A WOMAN'S INFLUENCE

It is no surprise that women are strong influencers for collaborative male leadership, given that the characteristics necessary for leading collaboratively are ones typically demonstrated by them. Men who early in life had front row seats in the struggle of a strong woman were inspired by their persistence, their resilience, and their grace in overcoming the obstacles thrown in their path. Sharing part of these women's lives, men came to embody those traits which served women in their struggle: respect for all, empathy, and a sense of shared accountability.

> *Men who early in life had front row seats in the struggle of a strong woman were inspired by their persistence, their resilience, and their grace in overcoming the obstacles thrown in their path.*

Patrick, our business unit president of a manufacturing company, mused, "I think about my career success and leadership in terms of who I am as a person, and that begins with my grandmother. When I was very young, my mother got divorced, so she and my grandmother raised me. I spent my summers and weekends with my grandmother and my mom's siblings, which included six sisters. The lessons in that formative stage of life—love, respect, work ethic, accountability—all came from that environment."

Patrick went on to explain that along with his aunts, he was expected to perform most of the household tasks: to set the table, to do the dishes, to do the laundry, to pitch in and pull his own weight. His sense of shared accountability took hold and grew then. "The matriarch of the family, my grandmother, showed the strongest leadership that I've ever seen. She had rules; she had expectations; and she communicated them always. She made it clear that we were all depending on one another, so we couldn't let each other down. I felt a strong sense of responsibility because she let me know I had an important role in keeping the family functioning. The good examples in my life were all set by females. I think that had a big impact on me and shaped who I am as a leader."

Emmet, our hospital system CEO, also credited his grandmother for being the spark and influence for who he has become. He said, "My grandmother was the church secretary and longest-serving volunteer in our local hospital. She told me, 'You will realize as you progress through your life, that you get more value out of helping others than you'll ever get alone.'" His attention to making others feel comfortable and respecting people throughout his organization reflects his grandmother's pearl of wisdom.

Stephen, whose organization coordinates organ transplants, told me that he has been shaped by female influence throughout his life, particularly early on. "I'm more comfortable with women actually. And this is a woman-dominated field. I was raised by a woman." He paused a moment and said quietly, "Yeah, my father died when I was nine." Then he continued, "I remember some of my mother's principles, particularly about being authentic, being who you are. She said to me, 'You can look at people, and they say they're religious, and they go to church on Sunday, or they go to synagogue on Saturday, and they're hypocrites. Don't ever be a hypocrite. Do what's right.' I think that's what I used as a model for how I lead."

Stephen went on to explain that his mother's influence gives him the energy and determination to fight for what he believes in, even if it means bucking the system. He engages people in that push by keeping the organization's mission front and center, creating a strong sense of meaningfulness, as collaborative leaders do.

Charles, our CEO in educational services, also credits his mother for his success as a leader, particularly in her lesson in continually reinforcing respect for all. He told me, "She was working full time, taking care of herself, taking care of her kids. But what I admired about her is that no matter how she was treated, she always respected people. Regardless of who you were, regardless of the title, regardless of pecking order, she respected you. My mom was always a kind person. She always valued an exchange with others. Watching her, that was my model."

Craig, our senior VP in technology, told me about a woman who mentored him right out of college and was the formative influence in how he leads. "She was the first female head of surgery of any major medical center in the country. She started the kidney transplantation program where my first job out of school was doing tissue typing. She was passionate about her work; no matter what, you had to do good for her patients."

Craig admired how she was able to drive for results yet be compassionate, even in the face of insults regularly hurled her way. "She dealt with a lot of sexism—from colleagues and clients, people who criticized her looks. She just sloughed it off. She was fearless, smart, and effective. She didn't get her way by bullying; she got her way by a combination of humor and intellect." He then joked, "She could quickly emasculate someone, wouldn't do it very often. It's one of those things where you're wounded, and you don't even know you're wounded until about five minutes later, and you look down and you go, 'Oh my gosh.'" After we had a good laugh about that, he reflected on her characteristics and said, "I didn't overtly model myself after that, but obviously it affected the way I look at being a leader. At the time, I didn't think of it as female leadership, just leadership in general."

LEARNING TO FIT IN

Several collaborative male leaders talked about being in the minority, not being a part of the dominant corporate culture. They always felt that they had to work to adapt to their environment or communities to be accepted. For some, it was the women in their early life that illuminated the way to navigate a world where men, mostly white men, pulled the strings. This did not surprise me. Women who are successful in their careers and lead effectively are attuned to their environment and work to fit in. As we discussed earlier, listening, reading the environment, being attuned to how people interact and react are skills that are important for leading collaboratively.

Men who grew up feeling that they were an outsider—be it by race, ethnicity, religion, disability, sexual orientation—have an appreciation and empathy for those outside the norm. They also learned to listen and pick up cues so that they could behave in a way that enabled them to adapt to the culture of the majority. For men who are a part of the straight, white, male

Men who grew up feeling that they were an outsider—be it by race, ethnicity, religion, disability, sexual orientation— have an appreciation and empathy for those outside the norm.

corporate culture, the concept of learning to "fit in" is a foreign one. After all, they don't have to think about it; they already fit in.

Stephen told me about his mother's influence on how he interacted with others, particularly those different from him. In essence, she modeled how to adapt and be accepted. "I was taught by my mom that you treat people the way you want to be treated. Sort of basic. I was Jewish in a town of Christians, the only Jew in my high school. So, you had to be sort of a chameleon to fit in, and I'm good at that, I always try to fit in." It wasn't that Stephen pretended he wasn't Jewish; he was just good at adapting to whatever dominant culture in which he found himself.

Charles, one of our other CEOs raised by a single mother, said to me that he recognized early on that every conversation should be a dialogue. "My mom always told us be open minded. Don't position yourself in a way that you're going to 'enlighten somebody.' So, I always walk into a situation quietly; she instilled that in me." Charles learned to listen first, particularly to those who had a different point of view, who were of a different race or religious background, and find common ground to have a conversation, not try to educate them on his own experience as a man of color. Tempering ego was one trait that allowed him to be open to listening to others, which he admitted was a constant challenge for him.

Patrick, who spent much of his early years with his grandmother, mother, and aunts, told me about his dyslexia and pushing to fit in with the other people in his class. He said, "My mother always drove me, always pushed me, and never let me sit back on dyslexia as an excuse. She never let me cut corners. She'd sit with me, do homework with me, make me hang in there with the other kids. I got tutored, but she wanted me to be part of the mainstream program and not spend all my time in special classes." His mother's insistence that he be in an environment that was "mainstream" gave Patrick the experience of making accommodations to be able to work with others.

Rafael had a few rough years when his family emigrated to the US when he was an adolescent. Not being American, having dark skin, being emotional, being overweight, and not being into sports all made him feel like he was very different. After some time of hanging on the sidelines, he eventually worked out how to adapt to his new environment, using something he learned as a young child.

He said, "My dad was a physician, and we had a very good life back where I was originally from. My parents wanted to instill in us that not everyone is as lucky, and we should appreciate what we have. So every year, it was our custom to spend time with those less fortunate in our community, to donate clothes and household items. After we came to the US, we went back to our mother country every year to continue that family tradition. I think all of these factors taught me how to be able to reach out and relate to people who are different from me."

For other executive men I interviewed who felt they were different from the norm, they learned as they progressed through school and career to be keen observers and align how they presented themselves and how they behaved within the

This attentiveness to others set them on a course of being an inclusive leader, being sensitive to differences, and bridging those differences through empathy and collaboration.

culture norms of a group. This attentiveness to others set them on a course of being an inclusive leader, being sensitive to differences, and bridging those differences through empathy and collaboration.

ALL IN A HARD DAY'S WORK

In addition to the impact of female family members, several of the executive men I interviewed developed their collaborative traits through their humble beginnings, often drawing the contrast between being working class and now being in an elite class. They learned humility growing up, and they tread carefully as they stepped up in social rank, showing they still had respect for those left behind. For example, Emmet said, "I came from a family that didn't have a lot of means, but we never really knew it. My parents were blue collar, and I saw how hard they worked. Then beginning with my earliest jobs, I chipped in, helping support my family and paying for college. I never expected to be in some C-suite position." Emmet's modest background shaped his pragmatic view of work; jobs paid bills. In his humility, he would never admit to aspiring to a higher station in life or think he could attain it. Many kids from a working-class environment have learned to be careful not to elicit the comments that come from aiming "too high" such as ,"You're getting too big for your britches," or, "Who do you think *you* are?" This certainly does the trick to reinforce humility and temper ego, essential traits for collaborative leaders.

Patrick, too, grew up with little in the way of financial resources and in a family with limited education. He said, "I was working in a restaurant from the time I was thirteen. I always had paper routes. I had to go to a Catholic school—my grandmother insisted—and I had to pay for it." He was also a first-generation college student. When he told his mother he wanted to be an engineer, she asked, "Why would you go to college and learn how to drive a train?"

Charles, like Emmet and Patrick, had limited financial resources and no cultural capital that college-educated parents can give. His single mom struggled to support him and his sisters working in what he called "a check cashing place."

A MENTORING MOSAIC

An interesting phenomenon I've noticed with most executive men I've interviewed or worked with over the last twenty-five years is the apparent absence of a particular mentor. Tom, the Fortune 50 CEO, told me years ago that a lot of executive men think of themselves as a "self-made man." He said, "Men get the CEO job and believe everything in their press release. They think they are—or should be—all knowing, no need to learn or get help. Women CEOs are more willing to be flexible and collaborative."

Tom was a collaborative leader who readily admitted that he achieved his standing through the assistance of others, and he was proud of doing for competent, intelligent people what other people had done for him. He wanted to impress on me that sponsoring, not mentoring, is what it's all about. He said, "Any executive who tells you they got to the top on the basis of their abilities is being deceptive. It's a lie. They got there because someone pulled them up."

As time has gone by, and I have zeroed in on other collaborative male leaders, I expected that I would hear more tales and tributes of mentors, of people who pulled them up to the top. My assumption was that men who are collaborative, who think about themselves as part of a leadership team, would also see their rise to the C-suite as a shared effort. This wasn't the case. And it surprised me that most of these men I interviewed, who indeed had a passion for developing future leaders and an enthusiasm for their own continuous learning, didn't reflect back on those who helped them, though some of them did.

Patrick, who credited his grandmother, mother, and her sisters as major influences, was one of them. He said, "Jack, who was a regional vice president, became one of the most influential people in my career." He described Jack as being like a father and giving him "tough love," saying, "He was a teacher and a coach giving me the right amount of direction, and asking me, 'Where are we going next? What's your strategy?' That's why he was such a great mentor. But man, you better have thick skin because he was a tough man. But as tough as he was, and this reminds me of my grandmother, he'd let me make mistakes, and he'd pick me up and dust me off and say, 'Okay, now go do it again.' If you listened and learned, put in the effort, and didn't make the same mistakes twice, he'd just keep working with you."

Jack gave Patrick the autonomy to learn by "taking the wheel." We saw this "giving them space to fail" practice demonstrated by two of the executive men in the Developing Future Leaders chapter. Collaborative leaders have their people's backs as they stretch their wings.

Emmet also talked about a mentor who actively sponsored him. He said, "I had a CEO who latched onto me and became my mentor, and I just progressed through the organization. I never really had a solid plan that I wanted to be a hospital CEO or health system president. I knew I wanted to work in health care. I wanted to make a difference and help other people. I just happened to have a leader that I reported to who said, 'If you're good at what you do and you produce the results that the organization needs, it's my responsibility as a leader to equip you with greater levels of responsibility and support you.' And that's exactly what he did for me." Emmet's mentor modeled the basic premise of servant leadership, that is, being accountable as a leader to provide help to people to reach their goals. This is something that we saw demonstrated in the chapter Cultivating Shared Accountability.

Other executives talked about a conglomerate of mentors from whom they could emulate qualities that felt authentic for themselves. Perhaps having several mentors or a series of mentors may have helped these leaders pick and choose desirable behaviors.

For example, Daniel, our CEO of a national managed care services provider, said, "I've had a lot of good role models along my life and career in the form of parents, teachers, coaches, bosses, business partners. I think you try to learn from everyone. You have to find your own style. I don't think you can copy people's styles, become something you're not. Ultimately, you pick up things that you see other people do, like the way they handle situations. But I've found you really have to wake up every day and be comfortable

> *"I've had a lot of good role models along my life and career in the form of parents, teachers, coaches, bosses, business partners. I think you try to learn from everyone."*

in your own skin. You have to find out and figure out who you are and what your style is going to be as a leader, and then try to see if there are things that you can learn from other people, refine, and adapt."

Our health system CEO, Neil, also talked about multiple influences and picking up different collaborative traits along the way. He said, "I had good mentoring. You don't grow up with a doctor father who is an oncologist and a mother who's a nurse and not be empathetic. But I have developed empathy more as the years have gone by. I'm more receptive. I attempted to take great characteristics of both men and women leaders that I've been mentored by, taking some of the things that I've admired about those female leaders and some of the things that I've admired about the men." He went on to say he also studied behaviors he did not like and made a deliberate effort not to adopt them.

Like Neil, Emmet told me about executives he had seen earlier in his career who he was determined *not* to emulate. "I saw C-suite executives that would come out of their office, walk down the hall, and not acknowledge anyone. They wouldn't even say hello." As we have learned, Emmet's style is to deliberately acknowledge people from all levels of the organization and express his appreciation of them.

BECOMING A COLLABORATIVE LEADER

What if you didn't have the influences that many of these men had early in life? Does it mean you are doomed to lead following the traditional male paradigm? Does it mean you can't develop the characteristics identified in this book that allow men to be successful collaborative leaders? Of course not; it does, however, mean exercising those muscles, such as tempering ego, empathy, and listening. And just as working out three times a week for a month or two at the gym doesn't build the strength and form of an athlete, one cannot become a collaborative leader by going to an executive education program from a nationally acclaimed business school. You may gain insight, which is important, but actually changing behaviors takes time, and putting those behaviors into action takes on-the-job practice.

What if you want to be a collaborative leader and emulate the traits in the Men's New Leadership Blueprint, but you are in an organization that is competitive, values superstars over teams, and promotes directive, non-collaborative leaders? Can you still forge ahead? Can you do what Vincent, our financial executive, did, who created a collaborative, trusting culture within his group while in the midst of a harsh, competitive company? Or consider Andrew, who is a leader in the cutthroat business of publishing. He coached people rather than directed them. Think of Patrick, the turnaround master who established reciprocal goals with his team. He got competitive individuals to come around to cooperate and trust him.

Whether you are a team leader, manager, director, or executive, anyone who wants to be collaborative needs people around them who are open to collaborating with them. Even in a difficult environment, it may be possible to create a pocket of functional collaboration in your work sphere. It doesn't matter what your level of authority is. People without direct reports can influence and collaborate with others.

Even in a difficult environment, it may be possible to create a pocket of functional collaboration in your work sphere.

What if you can't get traction and build collaboration around you in your current organization? Think of it this way: you will be developing these critical skills as future capital.

STRATEGIES FOR DEVELOPMENT

Having a powerful mentor who is a collaborative leader is perhaps the most important vehicle for leadership development. The collaborative leaders featured in this book are actively developing collaborative leaders. They are creating cultures where collaborative leadership thrives. Finding these mentors is desirable for a number of reasons. First, being powerful, they are in a position to be a sponsor, pulling mentees up through the organization. Second, their collaborative style has been rewarded and recognized, allowing them to rise to the top tier of the organization. This is an indication that leading collaboratively is supported and part of the culture. Finally, mentors can model the behaviors of the Men's New Leadership Blueprint in the context of their own environment. This profile of characteristics provides examples as a guide, but it is mentors who can offer a customized map.

Working with a coach provides a great opportunity to assess which collaborative leadership behaviors are your strengths and which are Achilles' heels that you need to strengthen, providing a focus and priority for development. They hold up a mirror, providing feedback that helps build self-awareness. Coaches also can identify the "unhelpful" behaviors that negate good collaborative ones

Coaches also can identify the "unhelpful" behaviors that negate good collaborative ones and the pressure points or hot buttons that lead to them.

and the pressure points or hot buttons that lead to them. By doing this analysis, one can formulate a targeted development plan, concentrating on behaviors to strengthen and those to temper. Coaches can give on-the-job assignments that focus directly on accomplishing those goals. Then, they can collect feedback from those who work closely with you—a boss, peers, direct reports, other business partners—to assess progress and get helpful input for you. Coaches may also suggest outside activities that can provide additional opportunities to exercise collaborative leadership skills.

Participating in facilitated experiential workshops—ones that target development of collaborative leadership behaviors—offers a setting where, by design, participants are collaborating with one another to learn and practice behavioral skills. Having an opportunity to try out actions and get feedback in the moment is a key benefit. As a result, these workshops often help form a support network that attendees formally and informally tap into as they continue their development journey.

People learn differently, and in addition to the interactive means described above, some leaders find books to be an excellent source of insight that will support their development. The trick is to find books that highlight the behaviors one is working on; it may take a bit of research to weed them out. Some of the collaborative male leaders I interviewed told me about books or articles that inspired them and were great lessons in leadership. These books were not necessarily in the business section either, but they told tales of struggle and ultimate success outside the professional setting.

One such book was *The Boys in the Boat: Nine Americans and Their Epic Quest for Gold at the 1936 Berlin Olympics*. Nick explained why he loved this book and shared it with his leadership team and facilitated discussions. He said, "These kids were definitely socially and economically diverse, so it was a story about how the coach brought these different beliefs together, and how they became one cohesive unit and beat the odds. I related it to here, and I said, 'We cannot be successful if we're not rowing in the same direction, all of us at the same time.' And I added, 'I see some of you using the paddles and hitting each other.'"

Rafael shared a Stanford Business School article, "DaVita: A Community First, A Company Second," a case study about creating a collaborative culture, with his new team when he first came in as CEO. He said, "DaVita had undergone a similar transformation to what we were going through here. They had regulatory issues. I gave my team an exercise to read the case study and then write me a report on how they felt they would fit into something similar, and how they would take steps to grow and evolve with a culture like that." The assignment actually initiated the evolution of the company's own culture change, one that Rafael saw as crucial to its survival.

Whether men are raised, mentored, or professionally developed to lead collaboratively, that muscle still needs to be exercised. The collaborative male leaders featured in this book had their own unique development journeys, but importantly, they carry on with that journey by continually learning and being acutely aware of their impact on others, their organization, and the communities they serve.

CHAPTER 11

Leading Toward a
Culture of Collaboration

"Culture is the shadow of the leader."

–Larry Senn

My journey to discover and share what makes a collaborative male leader began with the understanding that today's organizations need such leaders. And the reason they need those leaders is because the culture they create—one that fosters trust, teamwork, and a willingness to think outside the box—drives innovation and employee engagement.

I also began this journey realizing the disconnect men face in being collaborative leaders, a disconnect they do not have when leadership is top-down. We expect men to be dominant and independent, which aligns with what we expect of top-down leadership, but it is not what we expect of collaborative leadership. Men have the challenge of balancing those different sets of expectations to lead collaboratively as a man.

As we now know, the cast of executive men interviewed for this book illuminates a unique blend of attributes that are distinctly male and collaborative. They temper ego, show empathy, listen, respect all, drive mission and meaningfulness, cultivate shared accountability, and develop future leaders.

Each of these traits has an impact on the culture, and it is quite different than the impact of characteristics associated with a top-down leadership style.

To understand the effects that these leaders have on culture and how they lead culture change, it is helpful to have a framework for defining and assessing culture. With a framework in place, leadership characteristics, such as those in the Men's New Leadership Blueprint, can be mapped to the cultural aspects they produce and compared with traditional male leadership characteristics and their impact.

DEFINING ORGANIZATIONAL CULTURE

Kim Cameron and Robert Quinn, in their book *Diagnosing and Changing Organizational Culture*, use the Competing Values Framework to define four different organizational culture types and attributes.[26]

Figure 1.

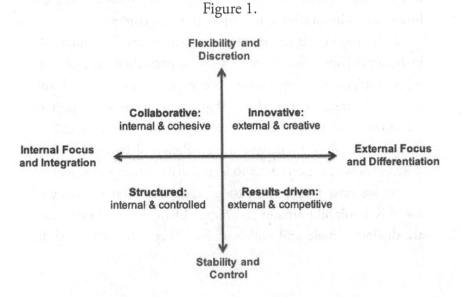

As the name suggests, the Competing Values Framework model depicts opposing organizational values at opposite ends of a spectrum where the vertical dimension is flexibility and discretion versus stability and control, and the horizontal dimension is internal orientation and cohesiveness versus external orientation and differentiation. Together, these two dimensions form four quadrants, each quadrant representing a particular set of characteristics that describe a culture type (see Figure 1). Organizations typically have some aspects of each culture, though often one culture type is dominant.

The Four Culture Types

Collaborative Culture is described as a warm, friendly place. Shared goals and values and a sense of "we" are woven into its fabric. What holds the organization together is loyalty and trust. A collaborative culture values cohesion and high levels of employee engagement and teamwork.

Innovative Culture is described as a dynamic place where original ideas are generated and executed. Authority flows from individual to individual or team to team, depending on what problem or opportunity is being addressed at the time. What holds the organization together is commitment to experimentation and idea development.

Results-driven Culture is concerned with getting the job done. Outpacing the competition, increasing market share, and generating high levels of financial return are paramount. The external business environment strongly influences the organization's strategy and structure. What holds the organization together is an emphasis on winning, achievement, and goal accomplishment.

Structured Culture is controlled and often hierarchical, with stable, ordered relationships among jobs. What holds the organization together is formal policies, procedures, and processes that create conformity and predictability.

Culture is created and maintained by leaders. Their behaviors and actions influence how people throughout the organization work, how they interact.

Culture is created and maintained by leaders. Their behaviors and actions influence how people throughout the organization work, how they interact, what's acceptable, what's counter-cultural, who is successful and advances, and who is "not a good fit" and leaves.

For each of these four culture types, certain core characteristics are valued in its leaders because they create and reinforce the principles of the culture. Some of the characteristics that are valued in one culture would be scorned in others. For example, a leader who inspires risk-taking is lauded in an **Innovative Culture** but would be considered a renegade in a **Structured Culture.** Leaders who inspire high individual achievement are applauded in a **Results-driven Culture,** but that individualistic success focus would be frowned upon in a **Collaborative Culture** where teamwork and inclusiveness drive success.

CULTURES CREATED BY COLLABORATIVE MALE LEADERS

You may be thinking, "Why did I need to learn about four culture types when surely collaborative male leaders create collaborative cultures?" Well, yes, they do, but the Men's New Leadership Blueprint, based on the executive men in this book, reveals qualities that are lauded in other culture types as well. It means that the Men's New Leadership Blueprint has a broad cultural impact, building collaboration, cultivating innovation and accountability, and driving results, but in a collaborative way!

Additionally, to effectively lead culture change, you need to understand the type of culture you are in so that you can "meet people where they are." One organization I worked with wanted a more innovative culture and hired dynamic, creative people into senior leadership roles to "shake things up." Well, they would come riding in on a sparkling wave of enthusiasm, only to crash on the shore. At almost exactly eighteen months after their arrival, they would join the ranks of executive outplacement. Being successful in that organization required being savvy of the current culture and taking that into account before trying to lead change. The organization's structured culture was conflict-avoidant, risk-averse, and rule-oriented. Moving toward a more innovative culture was like pushing a boulder uphill.

> *To effectively lead culture change, you need to understand the type of culture you are in so that you can "meet people where they are."*

How Tempering Ego Creates a Collaborative and Innovative Culture

As we have discussed, tempering ego paves the way for other critical characteristics such as empathy, listening, and respecting all, which are crucial to relationship building, establishing trust, and developing others. It enables humility, a comfort with showing vulnerability, and self-awareness, which make leaders more approachable. Without tempering their ego, leaders cannot see beyond themselves to connect and relate to others.

Remember Kevin who, in working with a group of physicians to streamline services, had to keep his own ego in check to let them believe they were running the show? He said, "It's less about my idea; it's our idea together. I can rest comfortably with that. I don't need the recognition." Kevin did a lot of listening, empathizing with the physicians who were facing big changes and sidestepping his own ego to help them feel more in control.

Then there's Patrick, who moved from turnaround to turnaround, building teams that drove company success. He truly believed it was these teams and not him that made the difference. He built trust with and among the team members by leaving his ego behind.

The collaborative male leaders I interviewed were well-regarded, accomplished, and, in some cases, a bit of a celebrity. Despite that, I did not feel uncomfortable or feel a need to prove myself as a professional. Their humility and the respect they showed me put me at ease. I particularly remember Andrew, the prominent publishing executive, who was so down-to-earth, casually greeting me at the elevator and instantly diminishing any status difference between us. In all of my interactions with these men and in the stories they told about leading, it was clear that they tempered their egos. They did not feel the need for recognition. As Charles said, "I have this office, but more times than not, I'm out there. I don't have the CEO title pinned on my jacket."

All of this makes tempering ego a highly-valued and necessary trait for a **Collaborative Culture,** but it also forms a trusting environment where people can stick their neck out and offer their ideas, which is a necessary condition for an **Innovative Culture**. We saw evidence of that in John's turnaround stories, his team members emerging from their defensive positions and offering suggestions as they engaged in problem solving. And Craig, our business unit head in information technology, also drew in his team. In his case, his three top leaders evaluated the situation of an impossibly late deliverable and "hammered out" a solution together.

How Empathy, Listening, and Respecting All Create a Collaborative Culture

Empathy, listening, and respecting all communicate to others "I care," "I'm interested," and "I understand." These traits engender connections and solidify teams, essential features of a **Collaborative Culture**. They are also critical for influence, persuasion, and engaging others.

Recall Nick, who regularly introduced himself to everyone in the company (often when riding the elevator to and from the executive floor), wanting people to know they matter and to humanize their perception of the company's executives. He wanted to be relatable. Kevin, who visited the women folding linens in the basement of one of their hospitals, was on a mission to express appreciation to people at the lower rungs of the organizational ladder. His demonstrative respect and concern had a unifying effect at all levels throughout the system. Vincent systematically and regularly reached out to people, creating a collaborative culture that he felt gave his financial institution a distinct competitive advantage in the industry.

Rafael, who says he "wears his emotions on his sleeve," talked about his empathy creating a work environment where people can openly be themselves, thereby working with more fervor. It created a **Collaborative Culture** that turned the organization's poor performance around.

How Developing Future Leaders Creates a Collaborative Culture

Developing future leaders fits a central principle of **Collaborative Culture,** that is, nurturing people's development. This characteristic includes the ability to recognize and groom emerging talent, and an enthusiasm for helping them grow. It also involves devotion to lifelong learning.

Dane and Vincent both could see characteristics in people that could be developed and deployed when others did not. Dane saw that Beth, who had been an Olympic coach and marathon runner, possessed the drive and the goal orientation to be an effective team leader. Vincent recognized that Jeremy, a candidate for unifying multiple acquisitions, was an orchestrator and connector, based on performance in another company. In both cases, they advocated for the leadership candidate and garnered the support of their colleagues.

Both Nick and Charles developed others by "giving them room to fail." What that really means is that they were able to step aside and let the people they were developing have autonomy to learn by doing. It's a collaborative approach, tempering ego and demonstrating trust and respect.

In another collaborative approach to developing leaders, Rafael expanded the senior leadership team to include two individuals from the next management tier down to enhance their development. In essence, Rafael made developing future leaders a collaborative effort with his direct reports. And by doing so, he diminished hierarchical boundaries and further broke down functional silos in the organization, giving more people "a seat at the table."

How Cultivating Shared Accountability Creates a Collaborative and Structured Culture

Cultivating shared accountability's team building, network forming, responsibility sharing, and inclusiveness are hallmarks of a **Collaborative Culture.** We saw examples of this—one from Andrew, who coached rather than "held people's feet to the fire" as his boss believed he should do. Another example is from Craig, who takes a "how can I help you" stance, believing that his job as a leader is to give people the tools and resources to deliver, not to micro-manage them. Similarly, Dane has a servant leadership philosophy of giving people what they need to succeed. We saw ample evidence of Patrick, our turnaround master, building teams by reinforcing shared accountability. And Craig, too, worked with his team shoulder-to-shoulder, having a "we're all in this together" attitude.

Meanwhile, cultivating shared accountability's behaviors around "holding people accountable," establishing shared goals, defining roles and responsibilities, and clarifying expectations are features that are critical for a **Structured Culture.** But the way collaborative male leaders do these things is, well, collaboratively. There is no cracking the whip or dictating, but rather, working together with their people to accomplish goals.

Hands down, the top role model for this aspect of cultivating shared accountability has got to be Patrick, with his very structured yet collaborative approach to "holding people accountable." He was charged with new teams in parts of the business that were in trouble. His secret to success was ensuring that there was clarity around everyone's role and how they were contributing to "the greater win." He focused on getting the group into a "cadence" where interdependencies around goals were established.

Another way that we saw our collaborative leaders hold people accountable was through a proactive approach. For example, Dane used a spreadsheet to systematically ensure that he connected with everyone in his network regularly, keeping up with them personally, but also with their progress on work projects. It allowed him to hold people accountable in a collegial way, what can best be described as *maintaining accountability*.

We learned from Rafael that cultivating shared accountability can also be a proactive approach aimed toward your C-suite peers and your board. He described it as building "decision capital," a comprehensive effort to surround yourself with people who are aligned with you and who you include in any decisions that need to be made. It means you are not ostracized and left hanging out to dry for a decision that doesn't get the desired results; instead, the network feels a level of responsibility because they were involved in analyzing the issues and making the decision.

In comparison, a non-collaborative leader would demonstrate this competency in a way that might be branded "driving accountability," keeping people on task and coordinated, but would lack the team building, network creating, and inclusiveness of cultivating shared accountability. Rather, it would rely on the power of authority. Non-collaborative leaders would hold people accountable, establish shared goals, define roles and responsibilities, and clarify expectations in a more top-down, control-oriented way, more befitting of the hierarchical nature of a **Structured Culture.**

How Driving Mission and Meaningfulness Creates a Collaborative, Innovative, and Results-Driven Culture

Driving mission and meaningfulness is yet another leadership competency that is highly valued in more than one culture. This competency serves as a mantra to loosely organize the individual passions and actions in an **Innovative Culture,** while providing a rallying call for achieving excellence and besting competitors in a **Result-driven Culture.**

For collaborative male leaders, however, this competency focuses on promoting meaningfulness where people feel they are contributing to a greater cause, creating a sense of "we." For example, Emmet believes his organization exists to better people's lives and used that as a unifying purpose across the system. Stephen united his organization by reinforcing their purpose to make life-changing tragedies more bearable for people and to have a positive outcome. Vincent emphasized his company's mission of building strong, positive relationships with their customers and with one another. It brought people in his part of the company together, and it attracted others who wanted to be part of a collaborative environment. Patrick kept the business unit's purpose—to provide high-end power solutions economically—front and center as his teams worked together to meet aggressive objectives in his many turnaround efforts.

Driving mission and meaningfulness involves not just continually communicating purpose but also nurturing and stewarding the culture to *reinforce* purpose; it is how these collaborative leaders achieve bottom-line results. Take Paul, for instance; the purpose of his business is providing a nurturing environment for underprivileged behavioral health patients, and he recognized that people in the organization had to experience a caring environment themselves in order to provide a caring environment for their patients. Tim also saw that creating the right culture to reinforce their purpose was the core of his organization's success; he believed this was achieved through his servant leadership style.

LEADING CULTURE CHANGE

Although companies see collaborative leaders as critical in today's economy, there are still leaders out there who are not collaborative. The cultural impact of those leaders slows organizational progress toward an environment that fosters collaboration and cohesive teams. Culture is the shadow of the leader. When you look at common behaviors of top-down leaders as compared to those of collaborative leaders, you can see how different that shadow is.

> *"Command and control" is the antithesis of flexibility and discretion, which are necessities for both Collaborative and Innovative Cultures.*

The old command-and-control, authoritative style of leadership drives a predominantly **Structured Culture** with a good measure of **Results-driven Culture**. There would be little to no aspects of a **Collaborative Culture** or **Innovative Culture.** This makes sense since "command and control" is the antithesis of flexibility and discretion, which are necessities for both **Collaborative** and **Innovative Cultures.** For that reason, it is a dated leadership style that is unfit for many of today's organizations and needs to give way to a fresh new approach, one that employs the characteristics of the Men's New Leadership Blueprint.

NEW LEADERSHIP FOR A NEW DAY

Leaders with an old authoritative style unilaterally establish goals for their teams to execute. The result is employees without a sense of control and often a lack of buy-in. Creative thinking is stunted when people are not included in the conversation about what results need to be achieved and how to achieve them.

Meanwhile, new-style leaders who are collaborative work with their teams to establish goals, giving responsibility to their direct reports to shape objectives and achieve them, and as such, they can optimize the particular talents and experience of their people.

Old-style leaders drive accountability by "holding feet to the fire," which can lead to a culture of stress, stunted performance, and disengagement. New-style leaders establish reciprocal accountability and help others accomplish shared goals, fostering a culture of high involvement, teamwork, ownership, and commitment.

Old-style leaders drive performance through challenge and by fostering competitiveness, leading to a culture of burnout, suppressed collaboration, and slowed individual development. New-style leaders coach and nurture professional growth to optimize performance, leading to a culture of continuous improvement, talent development, and mentoring.

Old-style leaders punish mistakes, taking away opportunity and support, leading to a culture of risk avoidance, apathy, and frustration. New-style leaders see mistakes as occasions to learn and encourage people to try again, leading to a culture of innovation, where people embrace challenges, try new things, and perpetually grow.

In summary, old-style, traditional male leadership in today's work environment disempowers and disengages people. It creates a culture of stress, choking performance. It promotes competitiveness, leading to divisiveness and burnout. It creates a risk-avoidant culture, killing innovation by punishing mistakes. And the emerging talent so needed in today's organizations has little opportunity to grow.

Collaborative leadership, on the other hand, creates cohesive teams and fosters a culture of high involvement and ownership. It creates a culture of trust, where innovation can take hold and flourish. It broadens and amps up the talent pool by nurturing professional growth.

□□□

The competencies of the Men's New Leadership Blueprint decipher the Collaboration Code. This collaborative leadership is not just the wave of the future; it is here now. It creates a kinder organization, one where people feel good about being there and want to do their best work. It is an antidote to the toxicity created by a still-too-common authoritative, egocentric leadership style. Collaborative leadership establishes a balance, and it begets cooperation, respect, and a broader perspective. It is a cleansing breath.

I invite all leaders to use the examples of the men on these pages to get on board and join the echelons of leaders who lead positive culture change and nurture tomorrow's leaders. You can make the world a better place to work and live.

REFLECTION QUESTIONS

As you read the chapters describing the Men's New Leadership Blueprint, you may have immersed yourself in the stories of the executive men, much like reading a novel. The examples are compelling, but what can you personally take away from them that will help you be a more effective collaborative leader? What can you do in your current role to build these skills? How do you build these skills and effect culture change?

The questions below are meant to facilitate your thinking in how to apply the lessons of *Collaboration Code* to your own life situation.

TEMPERING EGO: REFLECTION

Developing and maintaining a tempered ego is necessary to create and maintain effective relationships. What techniques could you use to enhance your ability to have effective relationships?

With whom at work do you feel able to let down your guard and be vulnerable? What is it about that person(s) that makes you feel comfortable? How could you provide the same feeling of comfort to others?

EMPATHY, LISTENING, AND RESPECTING ALL: REFLECTION

Jamil Zaki describes three types of empathy: cognitive, emotional, and empathetic concern. How would you describe your ability with each of these and with which type do you most struggle?

Who in this chapter did you feel demonstrated empathy and listening in a way you could emulate? What did they do?

Who could be a resource to help you understand your emotional landscapes… at work… at home? With whom could you debrief after interactions or meetings to help you interpret the reactions of others?

DRIVING MISSION AND MEANINGFULNESS: REFLECTION

As a leader, what intentional steps could you take to create a shared sense of purpose with your employees in order to steer your organization's mission and, thereby, fuel organizational success?

How do you define your personal "why" in your role as a leader? How does that align with the purpose of your organization or work group?

What role does the effective use of stories play in your communication efforts? What stories can you tell that highlight key points you want to make and want to make memorable?

CULTIVATING SHARED ACCOUNTABILITY: REFLECTION

Who in this chapter did you feel demonstrated cultivating shared accountability in a way you could emulate? What did they do that you thought would be effective for you, and what steps could you take to make that style your own?

As you think about goals you are pursuing, are there others who have an interest in seeing the goal achieved? Could you discuss with them what they might be able to do to help you get it done? How might you be able to support their efforts?

DEVELOPING FUTURE LEADERS: REFLECTION

How would those you lead describe your intentional efforts to develop the skills and abilities of your leadership team? Do they see you as a source of support and learning? Do they feel they can make mistakes and learn from them on your watch? How do you encourage learning and development efforts for them?

Personal development is a lifelong journey. The executives in this book would tell you so. The culture change that you can lead is also a journey. You can nudge the evolution of culture a step or two at a time. It is a slow process. Never stop learning; never stop pushing for positive culture change. As collaborators, we are all depending on one another to stay on the journey and make a better environment where we work and where we live. I think we will.

FOR MORE DEVELOPMENT RESOURCES

Please visit our website TalentStrategyPartners.com.

TALENT STRATEGY PARTNERS

Talent Strategy Partners is a leadership development firm established in 2001 that helps organizations, across the country and in all industries, accelerate business results by identifying and developing their emerging leaders—those who will create the right culture and desired results. We work collaboratively with our clients to understand the behaviors that drive their business and to build a robust leadership pipeline aligned with their strategy. Our work has resulted in companies strengthening strategically important aspects of their culture, being able to retain their best talent and promote from within the organization.

CHAPTER NOTES

Chapter 1

1. "CEOs' curbed confidence spells caution," 22nd Annual Global CEO Survey, PWC, 2019, p.31.
2. The Conference Board Annual Business Leaders Survey, 2019.
3. Gerzema, J. and D'Antonio, M. *The Athena Doctrine: How Women (and the Men Who Think Like Them) Will Rule the Future* (San Francisco: Jossey-Bass, 2013).

Chapter 2

4. Mayer, D.M. "How Men Get Penalized for Straying from Masculine Norms." *Harvard Business Review,* October 8, 2018.
5. "The design of everyday men: A new lens for gender equality progress," Deloitte Insights, 2019.

Chapter 5

6. Collins, J. *Good to Great: Why Some Companies Make the Lead and Others Don't* (New York: Harper Business, 2001).
7. Edmondson, A. *Teaming: How Organizations Learn, Innovate, and Compete in the Knowledge Economy* (San Francisco: Jossey Bass/Pfeiffer, 2014).
8. Reiner, A. *Better Boys, Better Men: The New Masculinity That Creates Greater Courage and Emotional Resiliency* (New York: Harper One, 2020).

Chapter 6

9.   "Women Poised to Effectively Lead in Matrix Work Environments," Hay Report, 2012. Hay Group determined that leadership traits like empathy, conflict-management, self-awareness, and influence were consistently tied to successful business outcomes within matrixed organizations.

10. Zaki, J. *The War for Kindness: Building Empathy in a Fractured World* (New York: Crown, 2019).

11. Brown, B. *Dare to Lead: Brave Work. Tough Conversations. Whole Hearts.* (London: Vermilion, 2018).

12. Riess, H. *The Empathy Effect: Seven Neuroscience-Based Keys for Transforming the Way We Live, Love, Work, and Connect Across Differences* (Boulder: Sounds True, 2018).

13. Goleman, D., Boyatizis, R., and McKee, A. *Primal Leadership: Realizing the Power of Emotional Intelligence* (Boston: Harvard Business School Press, 2002).

14. Boyatizis, R. and McKee, A. *Resonant Leadership: Renewing Yourself and Connecting with Others Through Mindfulness, Hope, and Compassion* (Boston: Harvard Business School Press, 2005).

Chapter 7

15. Wolff, M. *Fire and Fury: Inside the Trump White House* (New York: Henry Holt and Co., 2018).

16. Sinek, S. *Start With Why: How Great Leaders Inspire Everyone to Take Action* (New York: Portfolio/Penguin, 2011).

17. Malnight, T.W., Buche, I., and Dhanaraj, C. (2019) "Put Purpose at the Core of Your Strategy." *Harvard Business Review 97(5)*: 70-79.

18. Coleman, J., Gulati, D., and Segovia, W.O. *Passion and Purpose: Stories from the Best and Brightest Young Business Leaders* (Boston: Harvard Business Review Press, 2011).

Chapter 8

19. Cable, D. *Alive at Work: The Neuroscience of Helping Your People Love What They Do* (Boston: Harvard Business Review Press, 2018).

20. Kantor, D. and Koonce, R. "Consequential Conversations." *Talent Development*, August 2018.

Chapter 9

21. Dweck, C.S. *Mindset: The New Psychology of Success* (New York: Random House, 2006).

22. Brescoll, V. L., Dawson, E., and Uhlmann, E. L. (2010). "Hard Won and Easily Lost: The Fragile Status of Leaders in Gender-Stereotype-Incongruent Occupations." *Psychological Science, 21(11)*, 1640-1642.

23. Eagly, A.H. and Karau, S.J. (2002). "Role Congruity Theory of Prejudice Toward Female Leaders." *Psychological Review, 109(3)*, 578-598.

24. Eagly A.H., Nater, C., Miller, D.I, Kaufmann M., and Sczesny S. (2020). "Gender stereotypes have changed: A cross-temporal meta-analysis of U.S. public opinion polls from 1946 to 2018." *American Psychologist 75(3)*, 301-315.

25. Ibarra, H., Carter, N.M., and Silva, C. "Why Men Still Get More Promotions Than Women." *Harvard Business Review,* September 2010.

Chapter 11

26. Cameron, K.S. and Quinn, R.E. *Diagnosing and Changing Organizational Culture: Based on the Competing Values Framework* (San Francisco: Jossey-Bass, 2011).

INDEX

reflection questions on, 167
succession planning and management in, 124–25, 131–32
tapping into broader data in, 121–22

G

GE (General Electric), 55–56
Gerzema, John, 6
Goleman, Daniel, 71
Good to Great, 56
Greenleaf, Robert, 104–5

H

Harris Poll, 6
Harvard Business Review, 12, 79, 92
Hawaii. *See* volcano men
"how-can-I-help-you" stance, 107
Howes, Lewis, 8
humility, 56–57, 58–60, 84. *See also* ego, tempering of

I

Ibarra, Herminia, 128
innovative culture, 153, 154
    driving mission and meaningfulness in creating, 161–62
    leadership style and, 162
    tempering ego in creating, 155–57
Ishiguro, Kazuo, 45

J

Jobs, Steve, 94

ABOUT THE AUTHOR

Carol Vallone Mitchell is cofounder of Talent Strategy Partners, a talent management consulting firm focused on identifying and developing leaders who nurture the right workplace culture and drive results. Carol received her doctorate in Organizational Behavior from the University of Pennsylvania.